You Say...

BY
AUTUMN MAYBERRY

Tellwell Talent
www.tellwell.ca

ISBN
978-0-2288-2747-4 (Paperback)
978-0-2288-2748-1 (eBook)

Revelations 1:19 KJV
Write the things which thou hast seen,
And the things which are, and the
things which shall be thereafter

table of Contents

Introduction

Psalms 26:7 KJV That I may publish with a voice of thanksgiving and tell all thy wonderous works.

This book was written thirty years prior, put to paper now. Impregnated with a seed to fulfill prophesy. This little light of mine, I am going to let it shine.

Revelation 12 KJV

And there appeared a great wonder in heaven; a woman clothed with the sun, and the moon under her feet, and upon her head a crown of twelve stars:

2) And she being with child cried, travailing in birth, and pained to be delivered.
3) And there appeared another wonder in heaven; and behold a great dragon, having seven heads and ten horns, and seven crowns upon his heads.
4) And his tail drew the third part of the stars of heaven, and did cast them to the earth: and the dragon stood before the woman which was ready to delivered, for to devour her child as soon as it was born.

5) And she brought forth a man child, who was to rule the nations with a rod of iron: and her child was caught up onto God, and to his throne.

6) And the woman fled into the wilderness where she hath a place prepared of God, that they should feed her there a thousand two hundred and threescore days.

7) And there was war in heaven: Michael and his angels fought against the dragon; and the dragon fought his angels.

8) And prevailed not; neither was their place found any more in heaven.

9) And the great dragon was cast out, that old serpent, called the Devil, and Satan, which deceiveth the whole world: and his angels were cast out with him.

10) And I heard a loud voice saying in heaven, Now is come salvation, and strength, and the kingdom of our God, and the power of his Christ: for the accuser of our brethren is cast down, which accused them before God day and night.

11) And they overcame him by the blood of the Lamb, and by the word of their testimony and they loved not their lives unto death.

12) Therefore rejoice, ye heavens, and ye that dwell in them. Woe to the inhabiters of the earth and of the sea! For the devil has come down onto you, having great wrath, because he knowth that he hath but a short time.

13) And when the dragon saw that he was cast to the earth, he persecuted the women which brought forth the man child.

14) And the woman was given two wings of a great eagle, that she might fly into the wilderness, into her place, where she

is nourished for a time, and times, and a half time, from the face of the serpent.

15) And the serpent cast out of his mouth water as a flood after the woman, that he might cause her to be carried away of the flood.

16) And the earth helped the woman, and the earth opened her mouth, and swallowed up the flood which the dragon cast out of his mouth.

17) And the dragon was worth with the woman, and went to make war with the remnant of her seed, which keep the commandments of God, and to have the testimony of Jesus Christ.

CHAPTER 1
Dedication

Mom bellowed "Autumn, come here my girl." My eyes moved from watching Batman and Robin on the colored tube television to down the hallway towards my parent's bedroom. Quickly I jumped up, skipped my way to see what mom wanted. Mom was sitting on the bed holding blue fabric in her hands, "Where are your clothes?" Mom asked. Covering my eye's as I said smiling back at her, "I am hot." Mom pulled me in and said, "Lift your arms." I lifted my arms and she pulled over a top. I stared down admiring the baby blue fabric, it had little baby pink flowers on it. Mom turned me around, pulled me closer, so I could lean on her as she put the matching shorts on, "Lift your leg." She said. I could not help but lean over and look at the shorts. "We have to go to Church, let me finish, lift your other leg my baby." I lifted my leg and mom slipped it up saying, "Ok, let me see."

Stepping forward then jumping around so mom could see, I watched her tilt her head from side to side admiring the work of her hands. I turned around, first left, then right, then stood on one foot jumping up throwing arms like a dancing angel, smiling as I asked, "Do you think I am pretty?" Mom laughed and said,

"You are a pretty little lady." She pulled me in, lifted the top so she could check the waist. It was a little lose then she ran her fingers under elastics on the arms. Studying it closely she then checked the elastics on my legs. She smiled, turned me around patted my bottom and said, "Go wash up so we can go." Watching me as I danced my way out of her room.

I pulled the step stool out from the cupboard and placed in at the sink so I could see myself in the mirror, admiring the made with love outfit my mom had made for me. Reaching over for my brush, not taking my eyes off myself in the mirror as I ran the brush through my golden reddish blonde hair. I was not liking the results, so I turned the cold water on and wet my brush. Mom came in and saying, "Here, let me help." I pulled the brush in to hug it saying in a determined voice, "I am a big girl, I can do it!" Mom held up a pink plastic barrette with a bunny on it, saying, "I want to put this in your hair so you will be a beautiful little lady." Feeling happy with her answer I handed her the brush. I watched her fight with her left hand as it held my hair in place, neatly putting the barrette in place. She leaned in and kissed my cheek saying, "What a beautiful little lady." I jumped off the stool throwing my hands in the air, dancing my way back to my spot on the floor beside my older sister Lisa to finished watching Batman and Robin.

My older brothers Dave, and Ken came out from their bedroom dressed up in their Sunday Church clothes. We could not help but smile and giggle, knowing that we had to try and be on our best behavior and sit through the whole church service and not do anything that would draw attention to us. Dave was the oldest, even though he is nine he still had to set an example so his smile somewhat faded, but he still showed a little bit of happiness in his little man persona. Yet still saying we better not misbehave. Mom examined all four of us one last time, smiled, clapped her hands together and said, "Ok, let's go." We all piled into the new blue station wagon and headed off to church, the church bells playing in the distance.

Mom held my hand as I skipped into the Anglican Church, I danced to the sound of the bells ringing in the background loud and clear, "I loved going to church." I sang. "Walk like a little lady." Mom whispered. Disappointed, I quietly followed the lead of Dad. He smiled and shook hands with other men in the congregation, saying "Hello." Nodding his head with a smile ear to ear as we walked down the aisle, finally finding space for our family of six, three rows from the front at the end. Mom let go of my hand, I grabbed dad's back pocket as he led us to our seats.

The noise of people talking talk turned into singing, I hugged dad's legs so he could not move. Looking around all the men had suits on, they towered over me, not wanting to look at them in fear that they will squish me if I do something wrong. The man beside us was very tall, the tallest I have ever seen, he was slim. His navy-blue suit hanging because it was too big for him. What once was brown hair was thinning and turning grey. His eyes looked down on me without turning his head. Pulling dads pants as I Yelp, "Dad, up." Raising my arms for him to see that I wanted him to hold me close to him, where I would be safe. Dad reached down and pulled me in, wrapping my arms around his neck, hiding my face in his chest as he held me closely, afraid to look at the man beside me.

The Priest started talking and we all sat down, dad held me and hugged me close as I sat on his lap, my back to the man beside us. I closed my eyes as dad held me, I could feel him kneel, then stand up, then he sat down, then he went to his knees again. The Priest preaching the whole time. Dad stood up and made his way in front of my family as they moved back so we could pass, mom at the end of the line followed as dad made his way up front.

The Priest moved his hands all around me, up and down, committing me to understand God's purpose for the world, to encourage me to participate in bringing about this purpose. The Priest looked at my parents and asked, "Do you understand and support this, as this child being baptized?" "Do you promise to encourage her, to support the local congregation and diocese though the gifts of time, talents, and financial resources?" I could feel the vibration in dads throat as he replied, "Yes, we do." Still clinging to dad, having no strength as the Priest gripped my right arm and leg, taking a deep breath in, then holding my breath as I was dipped like a glorious banana in a chocolate fondue. I could feel myself gasping for air as I swung my free arm and leg. The Priests muffled words, "I baptize you in the name of the Father and of the son and of the holy spirit."

Finally, up for air as the Priest held me high before the congregation, firmly placing me down as if to say I am yet a babe, waiting to fulfill my purpose. Standing there soaking wet, water dripping to floor, ironically my face said it all, not sure if I should laugh or cry. Unaware of the road ahead as a believer in God, yet the love I would come to know and understand.

Suddenly my arms crossed to the opposite side, the sudden need to move the elastics on the arms and legs became unbearable because of the tension of the new role that has been bestowed upon me, one I did not understand. Looking to see the redness and restriction caused by the elastics, and water touching my skin, like I have grown. Yelping "Mom!" As I felt the sting. Mom quickly wisped me up in her arms saying, "It's OK my girl, mom has got you, it is going to be ok." My little arms were clenched tightly around her neck, my legs skinny legs gripping around her waist as she walked quickly to the wagon parked out front.

I sat in the back seat waiting and watching for my family as they made their way to the car. Lisa sat beside me, she was so pretty, turned heads all the time with her dark blonde curly hair down to her waist, her sapphire blue eyes softened when she saw me. Then Ken got in, he had a smile that you would remember, only one that showed we were metis, handsome boy, never wanted to be around me though. Dave, being last sat at the opposite window. His dark eyes always serious, his face softened when he checked to see if I was ok, even if he did not feel like it. My eyes started to close on the short ride home, it was an exhausting day. My head bobbing side to side, being so tired I could not hold my head up. Thankfully, I felt myself being wisped up, somewhat aware that I was being carried into the house and put into bed for my nap.

Rubbing my eye's as I sat up from my peaceful sleep, realizing I was not wearing the outfit mom made for me. It was fine with me; the long hot summer days were too much for me to tolerate anyways. There was no noise in the house so crawled out of bed and slipped through the crack in the door and staggered down the hallway, the smell passed under my nose as I closed my eyes, taking a deep breath in. Mom sang, "Awe me, did you have a good sleep my girl?" Suddenly I started skipping and running towards mom, jumping as she put her arms out for me, flinging me up to hold me tightly as hugged me. My head resting on her shoulder as my eyes looked around to see my family, they were not around. Lifting my head to get a better look for them as the front door swung open.

Mom put me down and I walked over to the door watching my brothers and sister untie their shoes, Dave and Ken kicked off their shoes in the closet, Lisa sitting on the floor threw her shoes one by one, into the closet. I was so proud of Lisa, she knew how to tie her shoes and spell her name, I did not know how. No matter how many times mom showed me the bunny running around the bunny hole, then finally burrows in, I could not make the bunny ears. Dave and Ken went straight to their bedroom, but I was not allowed in there without their permission. I begged, "Can I come?" "No!" Ken darted at me as he closed the bedroom door behind him. Lisa was already gone to our bedroom, determined to play with someone I turned quickly and ran.

Lisa and I had bunk beds, she got the top bunk and I got the bottom. Lisa was sitting on her bed when I got there. I stood on my tiptoes from my bed and peeked my head to look at her asking, "Can I come up?" Lisa quickly said, "No, I don't want you to pee on my bed." "I won't pee on your bed, I promise." I said kind of embarrassed. Lisa quickly said, "no." I dangled my legs as my hands gripped the top bunk, "ouch!" I cried because I banged my ankles on the frame. Letting go, falling on my bottom, pouting as I rubbed my ankles, not getting the attention I hoped from Lisa as she sat there ignoring me.

Standing up, leaving to find comfort with mom. Mom asked when I came in the kitchen, "What happened my girl?" My lips curled up, I stuttered, "I ba ba ba banged my legs on the be be bed." Mom came and picked me up, walked to the kitchen table and sat down saying. "Awe me, let's see." She gently lifted my leg and I point to the spot. Mom started kissing it asking, "Where, right there, and there, is that better?" smiling while I lifted my other leg, she quickly kissed my other leg stating, "Mom will fix it up all nice." Kissing my cheek, putting me on my feet, "Go play."

Going straight to the entryway closet I found my new shoes that had the laces, sat down, and put them on. Pulling the laces to see them clearly, telling my fingers, "Make a bunny ear." My arms fully extended as I carved a circle around the ear, thinking now what, confused, I cannot see the bunny hole. "Mom, I can't see the bunny hole." I said frustrated. Mom bent over and said, "Your shoes are on the wrong feet." I tilted my head staring my feet. Mom sat down and placed me on her lap and said, "Look my girl." Holding her hands by my feet. Unsure of what I was looking at mom placed her left hand on my left foot saying, "Left." Then placed her right hand on my right foot and said, "Right, see how they straight, the direction you walk, not toes pointing in opposite directions, your legs will walk right off your body." All I could do was giggle.

Mom took my shoes off, putting them on the correct feet saying, "See my girl." I studied the shoes; they did look like the way Lisa's shoes were when she wore hers. Looking up at mom smiling, saying, "I see." Mom took my shoelaces saying, "This is the bunny, this is the bunny running around the bunny hole, then finally burrows in." Once the shoes were tied, I untied them stating. "My turn." Mom patiently held me as my fingers tried and tried to tie my shoes, finally saying, "that is good for today." Mom sat me on the floor, reached in the closet and grabbed my other shoes with the Velcro, quickly changing my shoes saying, "There."

Jumping to my feet, running down the hall excitedly, pushing our bedroom door open, jumping up and down asking Lisa, "Do you want to play?" Lisa slid off the top bunk and landed on her feet like it was no big deal shrugging her shoulders as she said, "Ok." Lisa walked past me, I followed her as she walked to the closet, put her shoes on and tied them. Lisa grabbed the door handle looked at mom and said, "We are going outside to play." Mom said, "I will call you when supper is ready." We bolted out the door, ran to the swing set and started to pump our legs to see who could go higher the quickest.

We screamed, "Ahhh, it's going to tip." Dragging our feet to try stop the swing set from tipping over. My heart racing, Lisa jumped, I closed my eyes whimpering, "Yikes." I could hear Lisa saying, "Jump!" Finally, I let go of the swing, unsure if I would land on my feet. I opened my eyes as Lisa came half running and jumping towards me, her eyes were big, in a high-pitched voice yelling, "Wah, that was scary, you landed on your feet." "yeah!" was all I could say, my feet would not move. Lisa grabbed me saying, "I am still scared." Our fear soon turned to laughing. "You should have seen your face." I exclaimed. "I thought you were to chicken to jump." Lisa quickly added.

Mom opened the door and said, "Come and eat." Lisa and I walked in the house and sat down at the table. Mom put supper down in front of us, my lip curled up, hesitation written on my face as I blurted, "What is that?" I pointed to the chunks of battered meat on the plate. Mom said, "Mmm, it is liver." I crossed my arms, turned my head away as I said, "I am not eating that." Mom tried to hide her chuckle when she stated, "It is good for you." "I don't care, I am not eating that." I firmly said. Mom was annoyed, she retorted, "You are not leaving the table until you eat it all."

Mom and I carried on for a few minutes, Dave said, "I am done." I turned my head to look at him, his plate was clean. Ken shoved the last of his potatoes in his mouth. Mom said, "Good job, put your plate in the sink and go play." Dave got up, Ken behind him. I turned and looked at Lisa. She stabbed the liver with her fork and heaved it all in her mouth, quickly leaving the table to put her plate in the sink, then disappeared. I wondered, how did they do that? taking a good look on the table, nothing there. I looked below their chairs on the floor. Huh, where did it go? Mom, looked at my plate and said, "Eat my girl." I looked down at my plate, "No, I don't want that." Not changing my mind. Mom went to the sink to do the dishes, "You are going to be there all night, I don't care." She said with her back to me. I sat there and sat there, my eyes growing heavy as I watched mom move around the house. Lisa had a bath and was ready for bed, I was still sitting at the table, my arm was now on the table holding my head up.

My neck was sore, not only did I not sleep because of the curler's mom put in my hair, it was also my first day of kindergarten. I kicked off my blankets, stood up on my bed and popped my head up to wake Lisa up for school. "Lisa, Lisa, are you awake?" I whispered. Lisa did not respond. "Lisa, I am excited for school, are you?" I said a little louder. Lisa opened her eyes, noticing it was still dark outside she pulled the blankets over her head and said, "Go back to sleep, it is not time to get up." I plopped back down on my bed, took a deep breath in and sighed. Throwing myself back, my head hitting the pillow and closing my eyes.

I turned onto my side, then the other side, I could not go back to sleep. Slowly crawling out of bed, trying to be as quiet as I possibly can. Creeping like a cat cross the floor to the door to turn the handle, gently opening as I squeezed through, closing the door just as meticulous as it was opened. Running to the living room, jumping on to the couch, I kept jumping, having the couch never happened, and I have it all to myself.

Dave popped his head through his bedroom door, looked back in his room to make sure I did not wake Ken. Carefully walked out backwards, slowly releasing the handle. Dave whispered, "You are up early, bet you are excited about school." My legs swung straight out in front of me, my bottom bouncing on the couch then landing on my feet singing, "Yeah, yay." Dave smiled saying, "You are getting to be a big girl, come on, I will make you something to eat." My skinny legs dance behind him as we went to the kitchen.

Dave pulled a chair up the counter, reaching for the big tin of peanut butter that I was not strong enough to carry yet. Put bread in the toaster, walked to the fridge and got the milk and jam. Waiting patiently finally, Dave placed my breakfast on the table in front of me. Happily saying "Thank you," Dave then made himself breakfast. Mom came into the kitchen, looked at me smiling, asking with a laugh, "Oh da me, are you eating breakfast?" Reaching for my toast, taking a big bite, tilting my head back smiling. Mom giggle, shaking her head saying in a silly voice, "You have it all over your face." I looked at Dave, he smirked at me, put the last of his toast in his mouth and left to get ready for school. Mom made herself coffee and sat down while I finished eating. Once I was finished mom said, "Go wash up and brush your teeth, you are going to school today."

Prancing down the hall to the bathroom, tasting the peanut butter and jam on my lips. I popped my head in the mirror to see how bad it was, Dave always made the best peanut butter and jam toast for me. Stepping on my stool to turn the water on, splashing it on my face shivering, it was cold because I did not like to burn myself with the hot water. Mom came in just as I was finishing getting ready for school, she looked around and asked, "What did you do?" Stepping towards her, ready for inspection, grinning, showing her my face and clenched teeth saying, "I washed my face and brushed my teeth." Mom sighed saying, "your clothes are on your bed, go get dressed."

Although I did not know how to tell time, I did know that it was almost time for school. Excitedly running down the hall screaming, "Lisa, Lisa, it is almost time for school, I get to go to school with you today!" Bursting into our bedroom I found Lisa brushing her curly hair, strokes were soft and gentle. She had her new light blue cotton dress on, it had a white collar and a thin strip of lace that trimmed the short sleeves. "Will you brush my hair?" I asked still excited. Lisa ran her fingers through the right side of her hair tucking it behind her ear as she moved towards me. She took my arm and turned me around slowly, so my back was to her saying, "Let's see."

Lisa started brushing my hair, I could feel her trying to get all the knots out in the back. She got to the side of my hair holding it in front of my eyes to see, asking, "What is that?" "It smells like peanut butter and jam." I laughed. Lisa said, "Go wash your hair, you have rooster tails all over." Running to the bathroom, not wanting to be left behind on my first day of school. I stared at all the bottles lined up on the bathtub, even though mom read to me all the time, I did not know how to read. Remembering what order mom used the bottles, I turned the tap on, tipped my head under the water and wet my hair. After I was done washing my hair, I ran back for Lisa to finish brushing my hair.

Lisa was surprised, "Why didn't you use a towel to dry your hair?" She asked. Lisa picked up the brush examining my hair. "You didn't rinse it properly, go and rinse it, use a towel this time." Stress out, not wanting to be left behind I ran back to the bathroom and started rinsing my hair. Mom came in the bathroom, I could hear under water, "why are you not dressed yet?" Mom finished rinsing my hair and wrapped a towel around my head, put me on her hip and carried me to get dressed, brushed my hair saying, "Awe me, you look like a little lady." I could hear my brothers and sister yelling, "Let's go we are going to be late for our first day of school."

Mom swiftly picked me up, placed me down at the front door, Lisa had my shoes ready and mom disappeared. My eyes grew big as I noticed a bag when she reappeared, it was hand-made, almost as big as I was. It was rectangle, bright blue fabric with horses on it. The front was closed-up with Velcro, I could see my drawing Pad through it. The two pockets on the front fit my indoor shoes perfectly, the hanger made it easier for me to carry, then I could hang it up at school. I squealed, "Wow, I love it mom, thank you." Mom smiled, Dave looked proud when mom kissed him, Ken tried to take off out the door, mom grabbed him and hugged him kissing his face all over, using the back of his hand to wipe his face. Lisa stood there smiling, knowing it was her turn next, mom pulled her into her bosom holding her tightly, gave her a kiss and let her go. Mom gave me a kiss, looked me in the eyes and said, "I will pick you up from school at lunch time." "Ok mom, love you." Mom watched us walk across the street and disappear on the path that took us to school.

The big trees that lined both sides of the path block the warm sun, there was not a cloud in the sky. My new bag was nice, I liked it, but I could barely carry it. I was falling behind fast. Dave, Ken, and Lisa were so far ahead of me that I could barely see them. "Can someone help me?" I yelled with a panic. I threw the bag over shoulder and the weight of it knocked me over. Shoving my shoes that had fallen out, back into the pockets. Struggling to lift my bag so I could carry it I heard a voice from behind. "You are going to be late, I will carry this, just try to keep up." Dave grabbed my bag and started towards school, I was almost running to keep up with him, he quickly took me took me to my class and handed me my bag as he said, "see you later."

Standing in the doorway looking at all the other children in the classroom, scanning to see if they had a bag that their mom made. A voice said, "Come and sit over here." My head followed the sound of the voice, there was a young woman standing in the middle of the four big tables set up in the room, pointing to a seat right beside her, where I could see everything clearly. Making my way to the seat, I dropped my bag on the floor beside my chair and sat down waiting, looking at the huge clock at the front of the room, scared that I would never be able to tell time.

School went by quickly and mom was there like she said. I ran to her, excited to see her but I also wanted to go home, school was hard work. "Awe me, how did you like school?" She asked curiously. Taking her hand and pulling her to leave saying, "Good." Once at home mom made me a grill cheese sandwich with pickles then put me down for my nap.

CHAPTER 2

Yes, Jesus Loves Me

Dad worked long hours, sometimes he was not home for days. Mom had supper ready by 5:00 PM, Lisa and I were in bed by 6:00 PM, every night, even on weekends. Springtime finally came and I wanted to go outside and play. Lisa and I climbed the big tree in our yard, climbing branch to branch, going as high as we could without the branches bending. We could see everything and everybody coming, leaving, and passing by, nobody knew we were up here. It was our little hide away, staying there for hours, occasionally hanging upside down like monkeys. Mom would call us in, we always knew what was next.

Sitting there, watching, waiting for something interesting to happen, Ken came running around the corner, He was out of breath. Running into the yard, straight to the house, the door slamming behind him. Lisa and I looked at each other, then we gazed at the street in front of the house to see what Ken was running from, we waited, there was nothing. The bark from the tree scratched our legs and arms as we scaled down. I jumped, my hands stopped my fall, not noticing the injury on my knees as I bolted to see what Ken was running from.

Mom was holding Ken, her eyes caught Lisa and I standing there attentively, wanting to take in the information that was just shared between them. Mom whispered something in Kens ear's, he turned and went to his bedroom. "What happen, is Ken ok?" Lisa asked in a worried voice. Mom replied, "Ken is fine, nothing to worry about, go sit down for supper." Lisa and I sat down at the table, watching mom go into Dave and Ken's bedroom. They came out a few minutes later, Ken's eyes were red, Dave had his little man eyes on. Unsure what to think, I sat there waiting, not touching my supper, I was not alone.

Finally, mom said, "Lisa, Autumn go and have a bath, get ready for bed." Lisa and I did not want make mom upset, quietly we slid off our chairs and started the bath, dumping most of the bubble bath in the bathtub. Lisa and I got in the tub and played with our toys. After a while mom came in, grabbing a towel, she told Lisa, "Come, my girl, night-time." Lisa stood up, mom grabbed her with the towel and wrapped it around her, kissed her cheek and said, "Go put your nightie on." I stood up and mom reached for another towel, repeating the process.

Lisa and I waited for mom in our nighties at the kitchen table, she entered holding the hair curlers in her hand. I loved it when mom did our hair, she would say, "What a pretty little lady, you are so special." As the caressed our hair with the brush. When she was done, she would say, "OK my girl, go to bed and I will be there in a moment." Lying in bed waiting, Mom gently carved my face with her fingers "You are so beautiful, I love you so much, you need your beauty rest, you are going to take the world in your hands and become whatever you want. When you wake up it will be one day closer to your dreams." Being married and a mom just like mine, were the last thoughts I had before my body drifted off to sleep.

My eyes popped open when I heard something. "What was that?" I whispered, jumping out of bed, knowing I was supposed to be asleep, quietly creeping down the hallway, peeking around the corner. "DADDY!" I exclaimed, running as fast as my little legs would carry me, jumping into his arms. Dad's strong arms caught me, throwing me up in the air and catching me. My arms wrapped around him tightly, not letting go. "My little baby princess." Were the words he whispered in my ears.

Dad was dancing with me in his arms, the grip was so secure, my head resting in his neck. "FRED! FRED! Put her down you are going to drop her!" "You are drunk!" "If I want to dance with my little girl, I will." Dad slurred. My head perked up. Mom held her arms up, quickly moving to take me out of his arms. Dad swung around, I was starting to feel a little scared, Dad was moving all over making me dizzy. Finally, almost falling mom snatched me out of his arms and held me tightly as she made her way down the hallway to my bedroom. Mom tucked me in, kissing my cheek saying, "Go to sleep my girl, night, night."

The house was quiet, dad was in the kitchen making homemade bread as I sat at the table coloring in the coloring book, he had just bought me. Placing my color down admiring the picture I just colored, "Look dad, I colored this for you." Dad was kneading the bread dough in the white, gigantic stone bread bowl that I only saw when bread was being made. I held the book up for dad to see, again saying, "Dad, look I colored this for you." Turning his head looking at the picture, sweat beading on his forehead, breathing heavy as he said, "Thank you, that is a nice picture." Carefully, I ripped the picture out and put it on the table in front of me. Dad placed a towel over the bread bowl and carried the bowl to the oven to rise, washed his hands and came and took a closer look at the picture. Smiling as he said, "Go put your crayons and coloring book away."

Proudly I took my coloring book and crayons and put them back on the dresser in my bedroom. I could hear the noise at the front door, running to see the rest of the family as they arrived home after being out for the morning. Dave and Ken looked at mom with pleading eyes asking, "Can we go outside and play?" Mom quickly answered, "Do not go too far." The door opened and they were gone. Lisa walked by me holding a little paper bag in her hand, following close behind her I asked, "what did mom buy you?" Lisa proudly responded, "Bubble gum." "Ooooh, can I have a piece?" I asked. Lisa opened the bag and carefully pulled the package of Juicy Fruit gum out. "You are only getting one." She said as she handed me a piece.

Shoving the piece of gum in my mouth I could feel my top front tooth was loose. "Look my tooth is loose." Showing Lisa, using my tongue to try wiggle it. "Yuck!" Lisa blurted through the two spaces in her teeth. Quickly I reached down to pick up my gum that had fallen out of my mouth while showing Lisa my lose tooth." Holding it up for her to see, "Ten second rule, right?" Placing the gum back in my mouth knowing it was my only piece. Lisa grabbed my hand singing, "Let's go play!" Mom stopping us at the bedroom door, "Not you Autumn, it is nap time." Lisa swiftly disappearing.

When I awoke from my nap dad was gone, the smell of fresh bread tickled my nose, still groggy I slowly asked, "Where is everybody?" Mom was buttering the top of the bread and flipping the bread out of the bread pans saying, "They are all outside playing, go and find them." Mom did not have to tell me that again, grabbing my shoes shoving them under my arms, running out the door. Dave, Ken, and Lisa were all outside standing on the street, all looking in one direction. I slipped my shoes on and went to see what they were looking at asking, "what are you guys doing?" Looking down the street, I could not see what they were looking at.

Ken firmly said, "Come on I want to get a closer look." Proudly I joined the brigade, walking straight ahead, side by side blocking any traffic that would want to pass by, we were on a mission. "What are we looking at?" I asked, not being able to keep my eyes ahead because I had to watch my feet, afraid I was going to trip over them. Ken stopped, yelling, "What did I tell you." Looking at Ken, his arm went up as he pointed. "See, I told you, I saw him yesterday." My heart sank, looking out of my own two eyes, trying not to cry when I asked, "Who is dad kissing?" Ken yelled, "Run, hide, before he sees us." We all ran to the side of the gravel road, hiding in the bushes, our silence said it all as tried to process what we just saw.

We could hear the gravel rocks hitting a vehicle as it approached, dad drove right by, did not slow down, did not stop at home, just kept driving. The words, "I hate him." Slipped out of Kens mouth. A tear rolled down my cheek, turning and looking at the others. Lisa crying, Dave's eyes watering, Kens lip trembled, he did not cry, instead he said determinedly, "She has to leave him." "Ken!" Dave said firmly. "It is true, he is mean, all he does is hurt us, she was crying yesterday, you saw it." "Ken, not here." Dave affirmed. Staring down at my legs, realizing the wounds that I sustained the day before, are now being revealed. "Is that what you were running from yesterday?" I asked in a pouty voice. The silence, echoing.

The sun was going down, mom did not call us in for supper, still sitting in the bushes not saying a word. "I have never been out this late, how come I have never seen this?" Finally, my own words enlightening me. The blue sky was darkening, pink, purple and oranges surrounded the sun. My eyes caught Dave's glance, my pleading voice begged, "Why have I not seen this?" "Come on, it is past your bedtime we have to go home." Dave said through a smirk, his hand covered my head, rubbing it playfully before he turned and led the troop home, helping us all out of the bushes.

We stood outside the door, Dave's hand on the door handle, the unspoken silence said nobody say anything, Dave took one last glance at us all before we stormed opened the door. Mom jumped; her deep thoughts gone; she was back to reality. Mom put her hands on her hips saying, "There you are." Dramatically her finger on her right hand pointed to the table, her high-pitched voice saying, "Go sit down at the table." I have been calling you for hours, supper is ready." We all quietly sat down at the table staring at supper, no of us had appetites. Mom forced a smile and said, "Go get ready for bed."

School just ended and dad has not been home for a while. Lisa and I sat on the floor watching TV, mom had the bath water running. Mom reached in her pocket and pulled some money and handed it to Dave who was sitting on the couch, with urgency in her voice she whispered, "Go quickly to the store and buy some bread, make some sandwiches and we will go." Mom rubbed the top of mine and Lisa's head, firmly saying, "Let's go have a bath, make you smell all pretty." We got up and ran to the bathroom, our clothes dropping as we both hopped in the tub.

"Woah, that is cold!" We both wailed. Jumping out just as quickly as we jumped in. Mom came in, turned the water off and put her hand to feel the temperature stating, "Goodness me." Mom pulled the plug to drain the tub, reached for Lisa and stood her in the tub. I turned to run but I was not fast enough, joining in with Lisa as we stood in the cold-water crying. "There, there, almost done." Mom said as she rinsed Lisa off. She reached for the towel, wrapped it her and lifted her out of the igloo, giving her a hug and a kiss, calmly saying, "Go get dressed my girl." My crying turned to screaming, mom moving as fast as she could dumping cold water over me. Finally, the covering of the towel and mom's arms wrapped around me instantly gave me warmth.

Mom carried me down the hallway whispering, "It is ok my girl." Gently placing me on the bed, Lisa was already dressed, she stood there watching mom dress me while brushing her hair. "Are you done with the brush?" Mom asked. Lisa handed mom the brush so mom could brush my hair. Mom kissed Lisa's cheek, then mine as she put me on the floor saying, "Go get your shoes on." Our eye's red, Lisa and I went and got our shoes on. Dave and Ken were in the kitchen waiting for us. Mom appeared quickly in the kitchen frantically saying, "Quick let's go."

Ken opened the door, "Awh, look at the puppy mom!" We all stood there staring at the black dog sitting on the steps that led up to the house. "Can we take him with us?" Ken asked. Mom looked at Dave firmly saying, "Go put the girls in the car." Ken's pleading words followed behind us, "Please mom, he is so cute, let us have him." Dave walked us to the street, then to the front of a house a couple of doors down. Dave opened the back door of a car for Lisa and I and said, "Get in." Not sure who's car this was, Lisa and I hopped in the back seat and looked out the window. Ken was running to the car with the dog in his arms, mom following behind him.

Ken placed the dog on the seat in the back, got in and Dave closed the door. Mom and Dave got in the front seats of the car, the car started, and we pulled away. I stood up on the seat and watched out the back window as our house faded further and further away, mom turned off the street and the house disappeared. Mom turned another corner, my eye's still piercing out the back window, unsure of what was going on. The small buildings soon faded; I could not help but feel a tear roll down my cheek as the landscape became wheat fields. Slowly turning my body around, leaning against the back of the seat as I slid down not saying a word.

Faintly I heard Dave say, "Wake up, wake up, we are here." Half asleep I crawled out of the car, standing beside Lisa, our eye's gazed at the tall building in front of us. Mom grabbed our hands and led us in the building. "Where are we?" asking in my groggy voice, still half asleep. "We are at grandmas." Mom said happily. "Grandma's!" I exclaimed, jumping up and down, turning to look at Lisa as the excitement spilt over us, Lisa clenching her fists. "Yay, grandma!" Lisa squealed. Ken ran and pushed the button for the elevator, the doors opened we ran inside, the doors closed.

The elevator doors opened, we stampeded out, running down the hallway to grandma's door. Ken loudly knocked on the door, making sure grandma knew we have arrived. "Come in." said grandma's voice from the other side of the door. Ken opened the door, grandma waiting right there to greet us all with hugs, kisses, and laughter. Being pushed to the end, I was last, I was also the smallest. Grandma lifted me up when hugged me, her sloppy kiss on my lips said I love you, after all the loving mom took me out of grandma's arms and put me down saying, "Go sit nicely and watch TV."

I could not watch TV, mom was whispering to grandma, my ears were attentive, but could not weed out the words being exchanged between them and the TV, I was being pulled in two directions. Interrupting their conversation, I firmly stated, "Mom, I am hungry!" Thinking, I wanted to know what was going on, how come I had a cold bath, who's car is that outside, and where is dad? Grandma floated out of the other room clapping her hands together, a smile from ear to ear singing, "Come, look and see what you could eat until supper." Her hand guiding me in the direction.

Leaving my brothers and sister behind, I scooted to the pantry, there was a lot of cookies, I could see. Grandma held up whatever she could, I stood there nodding my head no because I already knew the packaging. Jumping out at me was a horse on the front, I always wanted dad to buy me a horse, "What is that I asked curiously." Pointing to the package. Grandma smiled saying, "You will like that, those are my favorite!" Grandma exclaimed as her eyes grew big. Reading her lips, every word she said, "Maple cookies!" Even though I was out of the regular routine, I ran to the table, waiting for the milk and cookies that deep down inside I knew made everything all better, though it was not, it was different this time.

Aware of what was really going on, sitting at the apartment sized table, dipping my cookie in the milk, knowing that the ones I loved were trying to convince me that things were different. My siblings soon joined me, our tummies feeling satisfied temporarily, until the substance of the real deal came to fill us. The doorbell rang and grandma scurried to the door, opening it, saying, "Thank you, keep the change." The door closed quickly with the aroma of Kentucky Fried Chicken following grandma as she placed the packages on the table, that being the only thing remaining the same, I knew something was different, my tummy wanted substance.

Smacking my lips, ready for a nap, I hopped off the chair and made my way to my spot on the carpet in front of TV. "Boring, is there anything else other than the news?" I asked annoyed. Lisa pulled me in to sit between her legs, knowing what came next, I sat there enjoying Lisa running her fingers through my hair, my head resting on her chest.

Remembering the events of the day before allowed me to piece together where I was when I awoke. My eyes looked around; grandmas bed posts always made me feel safe, this was not new. Sleeping beside her was the most comforting thing for me when I knew things were not right, she was not there. Being too small, I had to slid off the edge of the bed, my tippy toes reaching for the floor. Grandmas dresser was right beside me, I reached for her brush to brush my hair. Seeing my reflection one side of the brush made me turn it around, my teeth are coming in crooked. It was metal with designs on it, maybe hand carved, I could not help but want to look deeper. Studying the brush, gently placing it back where I found it. Exploring the rest of the things on her dresser, it was spotless, strategically placed, I felt so aware.

It was so quiet that my attention wanted to see where everybody was, as I approached the door, I could hear the TV, Lisa was sitting on the floor watching it. "Where is everyone?" I asked. "They went to go look at a house." Lisa said without taking her eyes of the TV.

Joining Lisa on the floor, we could hear voices getting louder in the hallway, the door opened, Dave and Ken were the first ones in. Grandma smiled when she asked, "Are you hungry, do you want to go eat?" Lisa and I both nodded. "Come get your shoes on, we will go out for breakfast, my treat." We moved quickly while Ken said, "I will go push the button on the elevator." Dave and Ken were gone. Once outside grandma and mom took mine and Lisa's hands to cross the busy street. It was scary, I have never seen busy street, I walked very closely to mom, hoping I would not get hit by a car.

The grocery store across the street from grandma's apartment also had a restaurant, grandma led the way and when the waitress asked, How many of you today?" Grandma proudly boasted, "I have my daughter and grandchildren today, for six please, and we need two boosters please." Waiting for our food Dave and Ken drew pictures while Lisa and I colored, my eyes grew big when I saw my pancakes with whip cream and strawberries. "Wow, I hope I can eat at that." I said with doubt. Time was of the essence, I had to show grandma that I was a big girl now as I dove into my food.

I wondered where we were going in town, I watched out the window, studying this new place. Mom drove through main street, up to the top of the hill past a huge brick building that was nicely landscaped with flowers everywhere. "What is that?" I asked with amazement. Grandma turned her head to look at me saying, "That is the Law and Courts building." The trees behind the building were huge, they lined both sides of the street. Mom turned off the street and drove a few blocks and turned again and came to a stop in front of townhouses.

Mom got out of the car and said, "Wait here." Closed the door and walked up to the front door of one of the houses, she knocked, the door opened, and she went in. A few moments later she came out smiling. Grandma got out and opened the back-passenger door and said, "OK, let's go." We all climbed out, mom said, "This is our new home." Walking up to the door I enquired, "Is dad coming." Grandma quickly said, "Let's go look at your bedroom."

I still had to share a room with Lisa, our room was twice as big as our old room though. We stayed at grandmas until our furniture got delivered. Saturday and Sunday mornings had more cartoons than before, the tv was beside the big picture window, Loony Tunes was on tv. I noticed a yellow bus pulled in front of the house and stopped, "Dave what is that?" I asked, Dave did not answer me and did not take his eyes off the tv, looking past me. I pointed out the window asking, "Dave, what is that?" Ken said "Quiet, we are watching cartoons." The yellow bus pulled away.

It was a hot, I stayed inside as much as mom would let me. "Go outside and play it is nice out, I will call you when lunch is ready." Mom said. I sighed, "OK." Lisa and I sat outside playing dolls in the front yard when I heard a loud vehicle turn the corner and was coming down the street. I pointed, "Look Lisa, what is that?" "It is a bus." Lisa said as she continued to play with her doll. "Where is it going, school is out for summer." Lisa shrugged her shoulders saying, "I do not know, church maybe." I watched the bus drive down the street and disappear.

Lisa held her doll up, moving in front of my eyes saying, "Autumn, do you want to play with me?" I smiled, picked up my doll returning the conversation, "Let's play." Dave and Ken came flying out the door, Ken pushing Lisa's head as they ran by.

We watched them run to the between the houses. Mom opened the door saying, "Lunch time." Lisa and I went inside and sat at the table, mom put down a bowl and plate in front of us. "Mm, Mushroom soup and grill cheese." I sang.

Cuddled up in my bed, I slowly climbed out, and crept out of the bedroom, I did not want to wake Lisa. Today was Sunday, I wanted to see where the bus goes. Dave ran pass me on the stairs, jumped on the couch and stretched out with the remote and turned the tv on. I walked to the couch and leaned against Dave, giving him a hug, looking at him inquiring, "What time is it Dave?" "It is time to watch cartoons, sit down or go somewhere else." He said meaning business. Moving as quickly as I could up the stairs, crawling on the bedroom floor to get my clothes, slipping back out.

Closing the door as quietly as I could, running to the street that bordered our yard, looking both ways before I ran across. Impressed with myself, stating out loud, "Wow, that was the first time I crossed the street by myself." I looked down the street to see if the bus was coming, there was nothing. Suddenly, I heard a rumble, the bus turned the corner, stopped in front of me, the doors opened, the dark-haired man sitting in the driver's seat said, "Good morning." Shyly smiling at the bus driver stuttering, "Mmymy sister Lisa, thinks that mamaybe you are a bah bah, bus that goes to Church." The drivers swayed his head when he answered me, "I think your sister Lisa is right, this bus does go to Church." Climbing up the stairs, taking the seat at the front of the bus I watched out the front window as the driver completed the route and halted in front of the brick building.

Holding the railing as I followed all the mom's making their way to Sunday school, tightly holding their child's hands, I joined the group of kids sitting in a circle on the floor, waiting patiently to get instructions. A few moments past, then a young lady with blue eyes, blonde hair wearing a dress, holding papers in her arms, started going around handing out the paper while she sang, "Yes Jesus loves me, yes Jesus loves me, yes Jesus loves me, for the bible tells me so."

I studied the piece of paper, it had a picture of a man beside a stone, wavy shoulder length brown hair, wearing a white robe. I could only believe that that must be Jesus, not lifting my eyes from the picture, the blonde lady articulated, "Jesus loved you so much, that he gave up his life for you, that his spirit dwells in you, you are co-heir with Jesus, because of what he did, gives you free access to God."

Sunday school ended and I followed the other children upstairs, making my way out the doors as I got on the bus. The bus stopped at the end of the town houses, so I backtracked to the house and went inside. As usual, Dave and Ken were not home, Lisa just got out of the bathtub and was combing her dolls hair to match hers. Nobody noticed I was gone; Church on Sunday's became my secret. I gave thanks before I ate, I prayed before bed, and before I got out of bed in the morning, I wanted to know this Jesus that loved me so much that he died for me.

The hard times were only what seemed a season, I believed that God would help mom and us. Mom came home one day, dropping boxes at the door exclaiming, "I have a job with the government, and we were accepted into Indigenous housing!" "We are moving into our own home, after five years of taking care of it and paying the rent and bills, I will own the property!" Finally, my own home!"

CHAPTER 3
The Devil's Dip

M om pulled up to the house, we jumped out of the car and ran up the stairs and waited for mom to open the door. It was a three-bedroom bungalow, Dave and Ken ran to the big room, calling it, "We get this room." Lisa and I ran to see our room, it was plain, but nice. Eagerly, Lisa and I ran to see the rest of the property, lastly opening the back door to see the yard. Our mouths dropping open, stepping out onto the steps, before us stood what looked to be a mountain. "Wow, look at that!" I exclaimed.

"That is Devils Dip, people have died on that hill while tobogganing." A voice said from the yard next door. Lisa and I turned our heads, on the other side of the bushes stood a brown-haired boy about our age. The boy smirked when he said, "My name is Brian, that hill is very dangerous." Mom opened the door saying, "I am going to register you kids for school on Monday." "Can we play outside, Please? We pleaded. "Ok, but don't go far." Mom said and closed the door.

Lisa and I jumped off the stairs and walked towards the boy as we introduced ourselves. "Can you hang out?" Lisa asked. The boy replied, "I will ask my mom." And disappeared into the house, reappearing a few moments later. "Let's go I will show you around." Lisa and I followed as he led the way to the front street, past a block, over the train tracks to the busy street, and stopped and pointed, explaining, "That is the school, that side is the old side, this is the new side. There was a fire, so it had to be rebuilt." "A couple of kids set it on fire."

Brian turned and headed back towards home, went on the side street, down the back alley and up Devils Dip. Panting when we finally got to the top, we turned and looked at the houses below, they were so tiny. Brian disappeared into the bushes, Lisa and I followed close behind. Brian started walking through paths, that went everywhere, jumping over trees that have fallen, leaping over dips, finally saying, "This is the brick yards, we ride our bikes here, it is a lot of fun." Finally seeing evening sun through the trees, we stepped out at the bottom of the hill. Brian said, "I have to go home now, my mom will be looking for me." Quickly we walked home and went inside.

Lisa and I liked the new school, even though we made lots of friends Lisa and I were still best friends. In the wintertime we would brave Devils Dip on our toboggans that mom bought us for Christmas, Nurse our wounds for days sometimes weeks. In the Spring Lisa and I would catch tadpoles from the ponds we discovered at the top of Devils Dip and watch them turn into frogs. In the evenings Lisa and I used to take turns massaging each other, we compared birth marks. I even counted Lisa's beauty marks, when I was done, she counted mine saying "Wow, you have a lot, I am at fifteen and counting." "Wow, I have that many beauty marks?" I asked her shocked. "Those are not beauty marks, there are moles! Mine are beauty marks, yours are raised." Ashamed, I moved to the side, Lisa moved on her stomach, I sat up to massage her back as she fell asleep.

Saturdays were always clean the house day, Dave and Ken never had to help. Lisa and I would watch Brian fly out of the driveway on his bike, then quickly move do the chores so could play. "I hope mom buys us bikes soon." Lisa sighed, "Me too, then we could go to the brick yards." I exclaimed. I notice my picture that I had hanging on the door was gone, I wondered where it was as I put the cleaning supplies away. Mom called, "Lisa, Autumn, come here my girls." Lisa and I went running, we stopped in the kitchen, excited, waiting to see what awaited. Proudly mom said, "Go look in the yard." We bolted, knowing that what we requested may be there waiting for us. Lisa and I spread out like an eagle when jumping off the stairs cheering, "Yay, we got bikes!" They were the same, cherry red, with a banana seat and a basket. Hopping on our bikes, we sped off out of the yard and down the street.

We rode our bikes to all four corners of town, eventually making our way to the brick yards, which became our favorite spot. Riding the paths on both sides of Devil's Dip for hours, starting at the bottom all the way up to the top. The only way to cross over from one side to the other of the pathway was at the top or the bottom, or you risk serious injury, maybe even death. Sometimes we would stop at the bottom and look at the dangerous path before, daring each other to do it. "I am going to ride down that one day." Lisa said proudly. I was not convinced; we turned and went home.

Lisa left early one day, I quickly hoped on my bike and caught up to her asking, "Where are you going?" Lisa responded, "To meet some girls that invited me to go bike riding." Lisa peddled faster, so I peddled faster panting, "Can I come?" "No, we can hang out later." Lisa said as she stopped, I did not notice Betty and Veronica in the middle of the street. I slammed my breaks. Lisa said, "Hi, are you ready?" Veronica asked in disgust, "Is she coming?" "No, she just rode here with me and is going home." Turning, looking at me firmly. Betty and Veronica turned up their noses, peddled their bikes and sat on their seats and rode away, Lisa rode off with them.

I stood in the street holding my bike, knowing that I was not pretty enough for them, that was why I was not invited. Lisa, Betty, and Veronica were tanned, had beautiful smiles, nice hair, new breasts. I had red hair, two different colored eyes, moles, and one breast. I turned my bike around, letting it fall to the ground when I got home, going straight downstairs to stretch. Praying, "God I Love you; I am glad I have you." Spreading my legs out, I reached out in front and realized my chest almost touched the floor. "Wow, I did not know I could do that!" I said as I looked up to God. I started doing other stretches, reaching to touch him, discovering that I could do the splits, the front, left leg in front and almost the right leg in front. I kept stretching getting closer and closer.

After a while I could hear Lisa coming down the stairs asking, "What are you doing?" I showed her that I could do the splits, Lisa tried, she could not do them. Proudly I kept changing positions knowing that I was better at it than her. "Do you want to go outside?" Lisa asked. Changing positions saying, "No, I am going to stay here and stretch, it feels good." Lisa went upstairs while I stayed downstairs stretching and praying, giving thanks.

When I was walking up the stairs Lisa was standing at the back door looking outside. "What are you doing?" I asked. "I am going to do it!" Lisa exclaimed. I looked out the door staring at the Devil, knowing what she was talking about. Lisa ran to the front as I followed behind her, she grabbed her bike running, then hopping on, peddling as fast as she could.

Lisa and I rode our bikes as high as we could up Devils Dip, our legs burning, unable to peddle any further, we hopped off and pushed them up three quarters of the way. Lisa stopped, saying, "Ok this is almost the top, far enough, let's do this." Still gripping our bikes as we turned around to see the steep, notorious hill before us, our heels digging into the ground to help us stay steady. "I will go first." Lisa said bravely.

Lisa determinedly grabbed both handlebars, straddling her bike, I stood there watching her! She was gone, halfway down the hill her front tire hit a hole. Lisa bounced off her seat, throwing her in the air, that was a perfect ten for her air handstand. My eyes were big as watched her. Her hands still gripping the handlebars, her momentum threw her over the bars to the ground, the bike flew over her, pulling her over the bike as it hit the ground. Lisa did not let go; Lisa hit the ground again, only this time at the bottom of Devils Dip Lisa's bike landed on her.

I looked up to God saying, "WAH! I AM NOT DOING THAT!" Turning my glance to Lisa at the bottom of the hill, dropping my bike, leaving it as I ran down, as I approached Lisa as she was crying loudly, "MY LEG, OUCH, MY LEG." I threw

Lisa's bike off, and helped her up, through her tears she cried, "My leg, it's broken, my leg." Trying to sooth Lisa I said, "You will be ok, I will help you home, grab onto me." Lisa put her arm over my shoulder, the tears did not stop as we made our way home, we got to the steps and Lisa sat down using her right leg to push herself up the stairs.

I hopped up and opened the door for Lisa, she jumped up into the house on one leg, her tears subsiding as I helped Lisa to the couch, I adjusted her leg, trying to bring her comfort. "ICE, ICE, I NEED ICE!" Lisa screamed. Running to the freezer I found a baggie of ice, grabbing it I swiftly made my way to Lisa's aid. "Submissively I asked, "Where does it hurt?" Long legged Lisa lifted and pointed to the lower anterior saying, "Right there!" I gently placed the ice on her leg assuring her, "It is ok, it will be fine." There were no signs of major injury, we iced for hours, we did not tell mom.

The next morning Lisa slept in, I sat in the living room watching tv, waiting to see how Lisa felt. The marks from the day before were prominent, the anterior aspect of her leg only showed the redness of a new bruise, the size of an apple, with concernment I asked, "How is your leg?" "It is good." Lisa said proudly, sitting down beside me. Knowing that now would be ok to mention, holding my stomach, I chuckled, "You should have seen what I saw, "YOU WENT FLYING TO THE BOTTOM DEVILS DIP! Ha, ha, ha, ha." I could see Lisa recall when she said, "Wah, that hurt!"

CHAPTER 4

Boy, What A Man!

B etty and Veronica did not hang out with me, when they gave
me the invitation finally hang out, I took it. I laid sprawled
out on the grass whining, "It is so hot, the shade feels good!"
Looking up to heavens smiling, I could feel the cool, soft grass
on my legs and arms as I laid there for what felt like an eternity,
with my eyes closed wondering what the surprise could possibly
be. Finally, they came out for inside the house. Veronica said,
"keep your eyes shut." Excitedly I closed my eyes tighter so they
could be sure that I was not peeking, a smile from ear to ear. I
felt something slip over my head as Veronica said "Ok, you can
stand up." I jumped up to my feet with anticipation, not sure of
my surroundings, I could not wait, I love surprises.

Suddenly I felt a push, then another, then I heard a voice
saying, "You are so ugly." Then I felt another push, then again, it
became nonstop, I was being pushed back and forth. The words,
"No one is going to want to be with you, look at you, who would
want to be with you?" "You are never going to have a husband, if
you do, he will have to be just as ugly as you, you are so ugly." My
world stopped spinning, my arms fully extended, I am by myself

in the dark, all I could hear was Veronica laughing hysterically. Pulling the bag off my head, Veronica fell to the ground laughing, holding her stomach. I turned my glance to Lisa and Betty, they stood there looking at each other, Lisa looked at Betty shocked, and Veronica was rolling on the ground laughing.

Holding my tears in, I turned and started walking, my feet got faster as my will and determination to get home was carrying me. I have never run that far before, my chest started to hurt my breathing was hindered, but I did not care. I had to hurry because the tears were wanting to flow. My legs burning, my feet gripped the gravel beneath me, the pain tortured me, I wanted to run far away. In the distance I could see Devil's Dip. As I drew near all I wanted was to conquer the evil that lurked on the scary horizon, throwing myself down to my knees, face to the ground, hands covering my eyes pleading, "God why can't they see?" My tears falling like a waterfall through my hands, shoulders shaking, I could feel myself entering the empty space where it was just God and I. Crying hysterically with a pure heart on Gods lap, "God, why can't they see, why can't they see I am pretty, is my heart right?" "Why can't they see me?" Questioning, "I am pretty?" My tears became an offering before the Lord, watering the ground beneath me, my sobbing did not prevail.

"I think you are pretty." Said a voice from behind me. My tears only stopping then, thinking, did I just hear that? Slowly turning to the right, wanting to see where the soothing voice came from. Still on the ground, with curiously I stared at the boy. He had dark hair and dark eyes, skin was tanned, only wearing a pair of red shorts with three white strips on the side. Gently he lifted his right hand to reach for me as he said, "I think you are pretty." His eyes met mine. He smiled, I was memorized, taking everything about him in. He moved towards me to help me up, the young boy became a grown man. His right hand placed in front of me to grab, my eyes studying his hand, I could not help but to follow the path up his arm up to the short-sleeved white dress shirt. His shoulders engraved in my mind, his neck small, being the only path left to go up to his face that imprinted in me. I placed my hand in his, not taking my eyes off him. He drew me in and hugged me tenderly against his chest. I moved my head back to get a good look at him, our eyes met, his face so soft and kind, reflecting his heart. I smiled, he returned the smile, it was exactly like mine, I was looking in the mirror. My heart at peace as I looked up to heaven saying, "OK." Then he was gone.

Following the path before me, stating, "I am definitely waiting for him!" Memorized as I made my way home, my voice could not help but sing, "Father, holy spirit, I love you… father holy spirit I need you… Holy are you God I need you…, now is the time God I need you!" Squealing with excitement, "Ah, I can't wait, I love you!" Twirling and giggling the joy inside screamed out, "OK!" Throwing my arms up in the air, not wanting anything but to be back in his arms where I was safe, he knew me, he is waiting for me, as I am waiting for him. Excited I screamed, "I cannot wait!"

Floating into living room, gracefully sitting down in front of the TV, turning the channels to watch I dream of Jeannie. Dave quickly stepped in front of me and change the channel to Star Trek, and stretched out on the couch. I yelled, "I was watching I Dream of Jeannie." Dave's eyes did not move from the TV, standing in front his view I reached to change the channel. "Change it and die." Dave firmly said, knowing I was not going to win this battle I walked out, leaving him to watch his show. Sweeping myself across my bed, recalling the beautiful smile like mine, the tender heart and the strong arms that sheltered me, I sang out loud, "There is only one worthy enough to be with me."

Lisa flew into the bedroom exclaiming, "Guess what!" Curiously, I turned onto my side looking at her, saying, "What?" "I got asked out on a date!" Lisa exclaimed. "We are going for taco's." Unsure of what I felt Lisa, she was beautiful and fit in with Veronica and Betty, for I knew that whoever I was with would have to like me for my heart, not my looks, that could be a very long time. Things were changing fast, Lisa had beautiful friends, going on dates, I knew I could not be a part of that aspect of her life, I felt like Lisa was embarrassed of me.

Lisa applied her lip gloss for the final touch, smiled at me, running out the door saying, "This is it, my first date!" The door closed and she was gone, I did not know what to do without Lisa, we were always together, she was always telling me how to do my hair, how to dress, what to do, how to act, I was ugly and an oddball, she knew it and I knew it. Wanting to know who this boy was, I followed her. I sat outside the restaurant and when I thought enough time had come to pass, I stood outside the window. The boy looked at me, said something to Lisa, she turned and looked, fury came across her face when she saw me, I was hoping for a different result, I fled.

Lisa was upset, I could not understand why Lisa was upset with me, I was her sister, her blood sister, I just wanted to be with her, why does she ditch me? Angrily Lisa said, "Look at you, you are just jealous of me." My heart sank, my eyes dropped down, no longer could I make eye contact with her, I knew what she was talking about, I was different. Staring at my chest, the tears started to welt up in my eyes. Unable to hide; I did not know, why was my right breast three times bigger than my left breast, why was it not there? My lips trembled as I brought my hand up to my mouth, knowing that my crooked teeth would be seen. Before I knew it, my hands covered my face trying to hide what was obviously ugly, I could not hide what I thought were beauty marks, Lisa called them ugly moles. I wanted my sister back, the sister that loved me for me and did not notice how ugly I was, the sister who saw my heart and was my best friend.

Stumbling up the stairs, running to our bedroom, looking on the door handle where my pictures hung no more. Throwing myself on the bed as my upper body shook, through my uncontrollable tears I cried to God, "Why am I like this, why can't I be pretty, why would you make me so ugly?" I cried and cried and cried to God, there was no answer, only evidence that I was crying. With that I lifted the weight of the burden I had to carry to the kitchen. Searching for a bowl with a lid so I could go see grandma, finally finding what I needed I ran out the back door, slamming it behind me.

Walking up Devil's Dip, for what seemed to be a million times, only this time my sister does not walk beside me. Once at the top I looked down at the houses below me screaming, "You are wrong devil, I am beautiful, GOD, SAYS SO!" Picking up the biggest rock I could hold, throwing it before running down the hill screaming, "I am pretty, he thinks so, he is coming for me!" Jumping over the dip that is known to overthrow the opponent, landing on my feet, turning, shaking my fist as I yelled, "I HATE YOU!"

Determined, I turned back around, walking towards the banks of the river where I knew I would find my comfort saying, "God

I love you, your will is my life, what you want, is what I will do, because you love me when nobody else will." shouting, "THERE IS ONLY ONE WORTHY TO BE WITH ME!" Noticing the raspberry bushes in front of me to enjoy, I climbed in picking, choosing with love, knowing that the perfect berry would bare the best taste in my mouth when consumed. Throwing a raspberry in my mouth knowing, that there was no taste, no words to described who he was.

Excited as I rang the buzzer to grandma's apartment, she met me in the hallway directly off the elevator. "Hello!" she exclaimed, arms open wide when the door opened, running to feel her embrace, yelping, "Grandma, I love you, I brought you something." She opened the container, seeing that I shook the raspberries to make her jam, just needing to add sugar to taste. "My favorite!" Grandma said, "Let's go and make some toast."

While grandma was making toast, tears filled my eyes as I sat at the table, "What happened?" Grandma asked lovingly. Whelping uncontrollably through my tears, "Grandma! Why am I so ugly?" Grandma pulled me in, moved her bible and sat down on her orange fabric rocking chair that I loved so much, running her hands through my hair soothingly saying, "God created you, God wanted you here, you were not supposed to survive, born on that sunny day, mornings first light, God needed you for a purpose, only to be revealed on his timing." Her strong arms held me as I cried, wanting answers. Grandma cried with me, "You are beautiful to God, he loves you and needs you to fulfill his will."

Sliding off grandma's lap onto the floor, the tears would not stop, soaking her lap. "Please grandma, please tell me what his will is, how could he use me, I am so ugly." "You have cuts on your arms." I heard through grandma's kisses, that soon turned to laughter as she tickled me. She kissed me saying, "God has a purpose for you, love and trust God and he will reveal it to you in time." Laughing through my tears asking, "Can I spend the night with you?"

Summer was coming back around, Dave joined army cadets and was away, Ken was never home, and Lisa and I were doing more things without each other. Only seeing each other in the evenings before bed. Mom made the house hers and seemed happy until one day when I came home from school, she was on the couch crying. I ran to her and hugged her, asking, "What's wrong, why are you crying?" Mom dried her eyes, shook her head saying, "Nothing." I questioned, "What do you mean nothing, why are you crying?" "Never mind, not for you to worry about it."

Lisa and I were jolted awake when the house shook, "We are going to fucking kill you." Were the words from outside. Lisa and I did not hesitate, we jumped out of bed running to mom's room. Leaping on her bed hugging her asking, "Did you hear that?" "SSSHHH!" Mom whispered. Curled up in the corner not making a sound, it was quiet. Waiting a few moments mom slowly moved off the bed, Lisa and I followed her, tightly holding onto her.

Walking past the boy's room I could see the shadow of Devils Dip through their bedroom window. Mom turned on the hallway light and walked further down the hallway to the partially lit house, stopping at the end of the hallway whispering, "Stay here." Lisa and I looked at each other scared. Mom looked closely out the window before turning the lights on in the house, making her way to the basement, Lisa and I whimpered, awaiting her safe return.

Mom came upstairs saying with relief, "There is nothing." We ran and gave her a hug and would not let go. Still scared I asked, "What was that?" "I do not know." Mom said. Looking at the clock it was the middle of the night. "It is OK, go back to bed, you have school in the morning." Mom said. "We don't want to go to sleep, were scared." Lisa cried. Mom continued to hold us tightly, walking to the living room and turning the television on, saying, "Sit and watch tv." After a while mom said, "Ok let's go to bed, you can sleep in my room."

The only evidence of what happened the night before was Lisa and I waking up in mom's bed. My eyes wanted to close while I sat in my desk at school, my head bobbing up and down. Looking forward to getting a good night's sleep, I snugged up beside Lisa saying, "I love you." Lisa hugged me tightly returning the feelings when she said, "I love you too." My eye's popped open unable to move, I awoke to heavy breathing on the left side of my face. I tried to turn over and see, I could not, paralyzed, closing my eyes praying, "God, please help me, protect me." The breathing stopped, I turned over and cuddled in with Lisa, drifting off, back to sleep.

The phone rang, stumbling to answer the wakeup call, half asleep saying, "Hello." "I am going to fucking kill you." Was the man's voice on the receiver. Thinking I was dreaming I repeated, "Hello." The words were loud and clear. "I am going to fucking kill you!" I did not hear mom come down the hallway, quickly grabbing the phone saying, "Hello." There was nothing, "Hello." She repeated. Still nothing, looking at the receiver before she hung up asking, "Who was that?" "It was a man, he said I am going to kill you."

Lisa was standing beside me at this point, her eyes were big, asking, "Who is that, why are they doing this?" Mom looking scared herself just said, "I don't know." Lisa grabbed my hand and held it tightly, looking at me not saying a word. Lisa and I held each other tightly as we fell asleep. Our eyes popped open, holding our breath, not sure if we should move when phone rang, lying there, waiting as we heard mom running down the hallway. "Hello." Mom said. "Thank you." And hung up the phone. You could hear the air leaving our lungs in relief.

Grandma came to spend a week at the house, she said it was because missed us and wanted to spend time with us, Lisa and I knew the real reason why she was there. It was quiet, nobody surrounded the house, there were no phone calls, I thought it had ended. The day Grandma went home, that night I thought the house was going to explode. BANG, BANG, "I AM GOING TO KILL YOU!" echoed through the house. Lisa and I ran into mom's room jumping on her bed, shaking as I said, "That was loud, who wouldn't hear that?"

Mom ran, flipping the light switch on in her room, quickly making her way through the house, making sure all the lights were on. There was knock on the door, Lisa and I ran to see what was happening, stopping at the end of the hallway, peeking to see. On the other side of the door we could hear Brian's mom inquiring, "What was that, is everybody ok?" Mom opened the door, Brian's mom's eyes were big, and she was shaking when she spewed out, "What the hell was that, what is going on?" "I almost hit the ceiling when I jumped!"

Mom told her the same thing she told us, "I do not know, it started happening a few weeks ago, we are getting phone calls as well." Brian's mom stayed up all night with mom while Lisa and I went back to bed, leaving when we got up for school. Moms tears flowed freely when she closed the door behind her.

The phone calls were becoming every night constantly, the banging was getting more intense, the police came by the house when it got closer to bedtime, answering the phone, "Town police department." The caller(s) would just hang up. Nothing could be done, no proof, being so I young I did not understand.

One day Lisa and I ended up at a home on top of the hill behind the law and courts building. I knew where Dave was, Ken has not been around for a while, never has been, mom stopped chasing him. I wondered where mom was, nobody said anything. Lisa and I were sent to school in a cab, going back to the home the same way. When school ended Lisa and I were stuck in this room together, I remember looking out the window watching the white woman as she tended to her beautiful garden.

Watching her as she walked towards the house, I left the room, grabbing the beautiful wooden railing as I sauntered down the stairs, reaching the bottom, finding the courage to ask, "Where is my mom?" The woman looked shocked, turned her head when she heard the question. Her face quickly turned blank saying, "Your mom is away, she is sad, she is depressed, she couldn't take it anymore, she is in the hospital." Her words making me stand taller, as tears filled my eyes, making direct eye contact with her, strongly saying, "Liar!" Turning, running back up the stairs closing the door behind me. Lisa and I did not leave the bedroom, we did not go outside. Looking from window on the second floor, the house was surrounded by huge, beautiful trees that caged in a beautiful flower garden below, it was very appealing to the eyes.

Lisa and I watched as the cab pulled up to the house, anxiously we waited, we are finally going to see mom. The cab was taken care of, we did not have to pay paid for it, barely stopping Lisa and I hopped out, dodging up the steps, almost kicking the door in to get to mom, hugging her, kissing her saying "I love you, I missed you." Mom hugged Lisa and I saying, "We don't have much time, we have to go." "Mom, we are home." Lisa said. Mom sadly saying, "We are moving." Loudly, I cried, "WHAT, I don't want to move, I like it here, I am not going."

Fleeing outside, running through the knee high grass, finally falling to my knees at the bottom of Devils Dip, dropping my head freely crying, "God please, please, I don't want to go, how will he find me, he will never know where I am." "God please, I am waiting, I promise I will for him, bring him to me, help him find me." Curling up in ball I laid there crying, "Autumn, Autumn." I heard from the house. Looking towards heaven, I wiped my eyes declaring, "God, I promise I will wait, help him find me." Lifting myself up, turning I started walking towards the house, I turned around one last time, getting one last good look at the notorious hill saying, "I know you heard me God."

Grandma was standing on the sidewalk, the bus was running, she gave Lisa a hug and kiss saying, "I love you." Then Lisa got on the bus. I was next, my tears started to fall, crying, "Grandma I don't want to go, can I stay with you?" Grandma hugged me and whispered in my ear, "Mom needs you, be strong for her, I will see you soon." Slowly I got on the bus, Lisa was sitting in her seat by the window, I sat down beside her as I watched grandma talking to mom. Grandma gave mom a hug, mom got on the bus and sat down. Grandma stood on the sidewalk watching the bus drive away, soon she was out of our sight.

The highway to the new city where were moving was long, and it was getting dark, my eyes were heavy, leaning my head on Lisa's shoulder whispering, "I don't want to move." Lisa leaned her head on mine, sharing my feelings saying, "I know, neither do I." We awoke to mom saying, "Lisa, Autumn, we are here." It was still dark out, the lights of the big city were bright, Lisa and I looked out the window until the bus turned off the main street, coming to a halt. Everybody made their way off the bus as we followed, we got in a cab, mom gave the driver an address that took us to a homeless shelter. Though the weeks have past, mom has lost her drive, she was not the strong, beautiful, full of life mom that we knew. Her bones broke very easily, she became scared. We have not seen our brothers since before the last month of grade six. Lisa and I was were excited, Dave and Ken are driving up and will be arriving today.

CHAPTER 5
Colors of Fall

One Thousand, Two Hundred and Threescore days later

My eyes popped open, I smiled as looked at the time, it was just before five AM, again I did not need my alarm. I sighed, "God, I love you, why am I awake so early all the time?" Being the only one left at home I said out loud, "First day of grade ten." I am no longer confidently ruling the jungle of raging hormones and awkward behavior of junior high, now I will be entering the battle war zones of popularity, and feeling the pressure of having to make a decision in what direction my life I am going to take. With the hope I would see some familiar faces that will give a comfort while wandering lost down hallways.

Putting my feet on the floor ready to conquer my first day. Brrr, pulling my legs back under the blankets, deciding that the comforts and warm of my cozy bed seemed much better. Snuggling up in my comforter, having wonderful thoughts of the one I am waiting for. I could not help but feel love when I said, "God, I have not forgotten, I am waiting." Believing this is the man that I shall marry. My eyes closed and I fell asleep, all in the comforts of knowing that one day I will give to him what only one would have, my virginity.

I jumped out of bed, oh no, I do not want to be late on my first day. Grabbing my clothes, I set out the night before, slipping them on after my shower. Quickly brushing some mascara on, stepping back to take a quick look. My flawless skin was tanned, I was dark, having a glow of a peach tone on my cheeks, radiating youthfulness, and innocence. Although I did not announce it, I was proud to be a virgin. Lisa said she was going to be the first in our family to graduate from College, I was going to be the first in our family to be a virgin when she got married, my thoughts spoken out loud, "God you know I need to be a virgin when get married, look at my flaws, oh, thank you for twos breasts." Digging in my bag, grabbing my coral lip gloss, nobody would even think that my natural hair was light ginger, with the touch of sun I put in my hair, it looked so natural, nobody ever guessed I was metis until they saw mom.

Running down the stairs and out the door to what was a warm sunny morning. Fall is my favorite time of year, what is not to love? The red, the orange, and yellow leaves twinkling on the branches before making their final encore until spring. Once they take their final bow, the musty smell and crispy crackle under foot makes me want to drag and kick my feet with all I have, just to get the beautiful aroma. This Fall I was turning sixteen, something magical was bound to happen.

Before I knew it, I was lying down in the leaves, it gave me such a feeling of freedom, beauty, love, and hope. I threw my arms out and swooped them up, the falling leaves were like a rainbow of glitter, watching them fall was like in a fairytale, just breathing it in, the sweet aroma of God reminding me that is glory surrounded me. Knowing I am already late for school I got up and walked to the bus stop singing, "I love Fall!" I just wanted to be outside.

Getting off the bus in front of the high school made me look to the left where I attended junior high, it was in the same field. The excitement of the first day was still in the air, the last few students were making their way to class. I have looked at my timetable so many times before, I already knew my first class was beauty culture. I was looking forward to learning how to do my hair and makeup, Lisa took the class and she always looked like a model, her hair was always beautiful and her make up looked like she was born with it. Walking down the hallway I saw the sign that said beauty culture.

Making my way through the double doors was mesmerizing, it was beautiful like a salon. It had sinks for washing people's hair, the chairs lined up straight. The mirrors were wall sized, pictures of models rocking the latest hair styles, placed there to see. I was so excited, I looked around the room, not recognizing anybody from junior high. I turned my head to the left, there was a girl standing there with shoulder length brown hair, big brown eyes, she was a couple of inches taller than me. She smiled at me and I smiled back at her, we stood there awkwardly. Finally, hearing a voice saying "Welcome, I am Mrs. Easton, I am going to be your teacher for Beauty Culture all through high school, grade ten, grade eleven, and grade twelve. I will be teaching you the basics of hair styling and makeup, by the time you leave here you will be well on your way into the fashion and beauty industry. But first let us start with taking attendance and we will then wash each other's hair and do a basic French braid.

After she was done taking attendance, she said "Pick a partner." I automatically turned to the girl with the brown hair and asked, "Do you want to be partners?" She nodded her head. We started to walk over towards the sinks she said, "My name is Nancy." I said, "My name is Autumn, nice to meet you." She picked a chair in the middle of a row and she asked me "Do you want to go first?" I nodded and said "Sure." I sat down in the chair and she put a cape over me and turned the water on.

I leaned back and Nancy started to wash my hair. The water from the spray massaged my head, I thought no wonder people like going to the salon. Nancy turned the water off and led me to a different chair to French braid my hair, after she was done, she held a mirror up so I could see the back in the reflection. Nancy smiled and said, "Looks good."

It was my turn to wash Nancy's hair. She sat down in the chair and I put a cape around her and started to wash her hair, she started laughing. I thought it was because the spray tickled her scalp. Nancy said, "You're getting me wet, really wet." I kept washing her hair and massaging her head, Nancy said "Stop you are getting me wet." I stopped immediately and turn the water off. She stood up and I took the cape off, she was drenched. Her whole upper body was soaking wet and her sweater drooped over her body.

I was embarrassed, I stood there with my mouth half open feeling stupid. Nancy laughed and said, "That's Ok." I thought to myself, why am I even doing this? I burst out laughing thinking nice job Autumn, first time meeting her, and you soak her. All we could do was laugh. She sat her down in the chair and I braided her hair, well at least that turned out well.

Lunch time could not come soon enough. Nancy invited me to the Mall for lunch, it was right across the street from the high school. Nancy asked, "What are you doing for lunch?" I said "Nothing." She asked, "Do you want to join me and a friend at the mall?" I said "Sure." As we left the classroom and made our way to her locker, there is a short girl with long blonde hair and almond shaped green eyes standing there. Nancy looked at her and said "Hi, this is Autumn, Autumn this is Patricia." We smiled at each other and did not say anything. Nancy said to Patricia, "Autumn is going to join us for lunch." Patricia replied "Sure." With a great big smile.

We walked down the hall together, out the doors, right across the street to the mall. As we walked, I asked Nancy and Patricia "How do you know each other?" Patricia said, "We went to junior high together." Nancy nodded her head agreeing. The food court was busy, so I sat and saved us a table. Patricia and Nancy walked up to Cockney Kids and ordered some fries and gravy, then came back to the table and sat down. We got to know each other as I shared their fries with them. Patricia was fourteen, even though Patricia was younger than me, we hit it off immediately. Nancy just turned fifteen in the summer.

We sat and looked around the food court, I did not recognize anybody. Nancy and Patricia had people coming up to them saying hello. Occasionally they would stop and smile at each other and giggle. We soon discovered that we lived in the same area and caught the same bus to school every day. Lunch was over and we went back to school for our afternoon classes, agreeing that we would meet after school and catch the bus home together.

After classes were done for the day I went outside to meet up with Nancy and Patricia. On the bus ride home, we talked about each other 's families and got to know each other a little bit more. I was the first one off the bus, then Patricia, then Nancy. As my bus stop arrived, I pulled the bell, smiled, and said "Goodbye." to my new friends and walked home. That was a good first day.

I lived-in low-income housing and I was embarrassed at the thought of even bringing my friends home to see where I lived. I walked up the stairs of my front door and opened it up. As I opened the door, I got smothered by the smell of cigarette smoke, it is kind of disgusting. Mom was home as usual because she did not work because of her disability.

Running straight up the stairs I turned the radio on, Prince, U Got the Look was playing. I started to dance in front of the mirror, then jumped up and down on my bed and pretended I was Sheena Easton, then collapsed and played the guitar. I heard mom yell through the noise, "Autumn, come here." I rolled my eyes and said, "Now what." I went downstairs and my mom put out a cigarette and said to me "Make me a coffee, eh." I mumbled under my breath "Why can't you do it yourself?" I quickly went over to the coffee pot, made her some coffee, put it on the table and went and turned the TV on in the living room.

Sitting on the couch, flipping through the channels on TV and found Much Music. I could hear Mom coming through the pass through from the kitchen into the living room, she looked at me and said "Autumn, I have no cigarettes, get me some." Replying, "I do not know where to go to get you cigarettes." I just started a part-time job at a corner store downtown, I sold Lysol to Lysol drinkers. All the money I made there went to pay the bills that my mom cannot pay out of her welfare cheque. Mom doubled up her fist and came towards me, shaking her fist saying, "Get me some fucking cigarettes." I always knew what that meant, and I thought to myself I better find her some cigarettes, I wish she cared that much about eating.

Quietly I picked up the hands-free phone and went upstairs to called Lisa. The phone rang, on the other end Lisa said "Hello." I said, "Hey how's it going?" She said "Good, how are you?" I said, "I'm OK, mom doesn't have any cigarettes and you know what that means, do you have any money so I can buy her some cigarettes?" There was silence on the other end and finally she said "No, sorry." I said "OK, maybe I'll see you at school tomorrow." Lisa said "Yeah, love you." I said, "I love you too."

Hanging up the phone I thought to myself, now what? Taking a deep breath In I sighed, saying out loud. "I guess I could call Dan." Dan was a friend that I met through Lisa, he always brought cigarettes for my mom when Lisa asked. His mom's boyfriend owned the corner store where I just started working part time to make money. I picked up the phone and dialed Dan's number, it rang a few times and then finally his mom picked up the phone and said, "Hello." I said "Hello, is Dan there?" She replied, "No sorry he isn't home right now, he is at work." I said, "OK thank you, could you please tell him that Autumn called?" She said "Yes, I will tell him."

I quietly went back downstairs and finished watching Much Music. Just as the show was ending mom asked, "Did you find me some cigarettes?' I said "No." Mom yelled "Oh, Fuck!" and quickly started to come at me, I stood up to walk away. She grabbed my hair and started calling me, "Fucking slut, whore." Swinging my head. I started to cry and said, "No mom I am not, I am a virgin waiting for marriage, I promise!" Mom let go of my hair and said, "Fucking Bitch, you better find me some smokes."

I wiped the tears from my eyes and walked over to the fridge and opened the door to see what I could eat. There was margarine, and milk, that was it. I turned and opened the cupboard and all there was jam, peanut butter and a jar of what looked to be spaghetti sauce but there was no label on it, so I didn't want to find out what it was. I closed the cupboard and said to mom, "I am going out to try to get some cigarettes for you." I quickly put my shoes on and walked out the door.

I ran across the street and when I got to the park I slowed down and let my tears fall freely. I cried out "God how long am I going to have to go through this?" "God you know my heart I love mom, but she is mean. I have a pure heart for you, I want to honor you!" "Please God I need you." I started walking towards the park pathway I did not know where to go so I just kept walking, I did a complete circle and finally found myself back at home.

I opened the door scared to what I was coming back to, mom was sitting at the kitchen table she asked, "Did you get me some smokes?" I said "No." She said, "Go next door and ask for a cigarette." I opened the door and hopped across to the neighbor's steps. I knocked on the door, Marty open the door and said, "Hey Autumn, how's it going?" I said, "It's going OK, Mom doesn't have any cigarettes again, do you mind if I borrow a cigarette for her?" He said, "Just a minute I'll ask." He closed the door. I stood outside waiting patiently, hoping that his parents would give me a cigarette for mom. Marty came back with two cigarettes in his hands and said, "Here you go." I said, "Thank you." He smiled and said, "You are welcome." Then closed the door.

I went back in the house and gave mom the cigarettes. She said, "Make me a coffee, eh!" Hesitantly I made her a coffee as she lit her cigarette. I said, "I am going to have a shower then I am going to sleep, good night." She said "Night." I went upstairs had my shower and crawled into bed. I closed my eyes and started to pray until I fell asleep. I jumped up to my alarm going off, I shut it off and turned over and snuggled with my comforter, it seemed a little colder I said, "God I love you, thank you for this beautiful day." I sighed and laid there a little bit longer.

The house was quiet, I got up and made my bed, then went to the washroom and came back to my bedroom and got ready for school. Once I was ready, I quietly started to go downstairs hoping to sneak out when I heard "Autumn, come here." I rolled my eyes and turned around back up the stairs and walked to mom's room." "Yeah." I replied. Mom said in a groggy voice "Bring home cigarettes." I said, "I will try." "You better." Mom said as a demand. I sighed, rolled my eyes, and went downstairs, put my shoes on and left out the door. I turned around and looked at the front of the house. I thought to myself, I cannot wait to be free from her. I do not understand her at all, how come she is different? I quickly turned towards the pathway and walked to the bus stop. The fall sun peeked through the branches of the trees; the light breeze twinkled each leaf daring them to jump. It was a perfect temperature, I needed a sweater in the morning, by the afternoon I carried my sweater with me.

I was the only one at the bus stop when I arrived, I sat down on the bench in the shelter. The trees lined the street down both sides and the view, breathtaking. I started thinking about my Fall wedding, the streets were replaced with green grass to compliment the fall colored leaves on the trees. There are chairs lined up, filled with my friends and family anticipating my arrival to be joined to my love that awaited me at the lit-up arch.

I heard the bus turn the corner as it approached the stop, standing up, taking my bus pass out of my pocket as I moved closer to the stop. The bus came to a halt and I stepped up, I didn't even make eye contact with the bus driver, immediately turning my glance to the back of the bus where Nancy and Patricia were sitting in the very back seats. I smiled and made my way back to the seat in front of them, I wanted to see their faces when I talked to them. I said, "Good morning." They smiled and said, "Good morning." Patricia was very shy, her green eyes looked like doll eyes, and she had lighter highlights in her hair from the summer sun. Her skin was tanned, she looked like a California girl. Nancy had a beauty mark below her left eye, her skin was pale and looked like she was inside all summer.

Nancy had a half smile, she did not show her teeth, but you could tell she was smiling. Before we knew it, we approached the Bus Terminal where we transferred buses to get to school. We got off the bus and Nancy took a pack of cigarettes from her bag and lit one with the lighter she had in her pocket. I asked, "Can I have a cigarette?" She took one out of the pack and handed it to me, lifted her lighter to light it for me, I said "The bus is here, I will have it later." as I put the cigarette in my pocket. Nancy offered me a drag of her cigarette, I said "No thank you, I will wait." Nancy flicked the cherry off the end of her cigarette and put it in her package and got on the bus behind Patricia and me. There was a lot of noise and the excitement of a new year rung through the bus. we looked around anxiously wondering if we knew anybody.

The bus started to pull out, Nancy tapped Patricia on the shoulder, pointing to a bus going by saying, "Look there is Bailey and Paige." Patricia leaned over and started to wave out the window with a great big smile on her face, hoping to get their attention. I turned to look to see who they were waving at, the bus passed by quickly and I did not see who it was.

Thankfully, we got seats, the bus was completely full, the bus driver did not stop to pick any more people up. I was embarrassed to look up because the young guy standing directly in front of me holding on to the bar above my head had his pants down just below his bottom, his underwear was in full view. I smiled and looked at Patricia and Nancy. They started to giggle, they knew why I was smiling at them, turning my head to look out the window as we headed off to school.

The bus pulled up to the school and we piled off, Nancy took her butt out of her cigarette package and lit it. I checked my pocket to make sure that the cigarette Nancy gave me was not broken. As we walked up to the school Dan approached me, Patricia and Nancy kept walking. He was a tall skinny Indigenous boy. He said, "Mom told me you called last night, sorry I was working and didn't get home until late." I said, "Yeah sorry to bother you, mom has no cigarettes and I was calling to see if you could bring some, I am sorry." Dan said, "Don't worry about it, Lisa told me how your mom gets when she has no cigarettes." Dan pulled his wallet from his pocket and handed me twenty dollars. I said, "Thank you." "He said "You are very welcome." "Hey, the church youth group is on Thursday evenings, would you like to come?" I said "Sure, let me know where and when." Dan nodded his head and said, "Will do, I have to get to class." "See you later." With a half smirk.

I walked up to Nancy and Patricia, they were just putting their cigarettes out and said, "We are going to class." I said "OK." I walked to my locker, and opened it, I grabbed my books and left for class as well. As I walked down the hallway I smiled looking around, I did not recognize anybody, I thought wow the big city sure is different than a small town. Where are the people I went to junior high with? After class was done, I went downstairs to different doors to see if I could find Lisa. I looked out the window and did not see her.

Even though Lisa was only sixteen she left because of the drama, mom always made her, and I do things even though she was home all day. Mom seemed different, she was not the same, but I still cared for her. The thing Lisa hated the most was how mom acts when she did not have cigarettes. I missed Lisa so much. Disappointedly, I walked down to the doors where Nancy and Patricia were, opened the door and they said "Hi." As I came out. "Hi." I said back. The sun was shining, I watched Nancy put out her cigarette and followed them both in. They headed upstairs to their lockers. While we were walking up the stairs Patricia asked, "Where is your locker?" I said, "Downstairs by the doors we just came in, the locker beside me has no lock on it, maybe you can take that one so we will be close." They walked right to their lockers and Nancy opened hers and put her cigarettes in the locker, grabbed her books and left for class.

As I sat down, I heard a stern voice say, "You are late." I turned and looked at her and said, "I am sorry." The teacher's expression was cold. Her brown lipstick accentuated her top lip curling up.

Her hair looked like it was just left after crawling out of bed. She was short, even with her two-inch heels, her black skirt was three quarters in length and her chubby legs turned her heavy body abruptly towards the chalkboard and said, "My name is Mrs. Galant, I will not tolerate tardiness." She tapped the piece of chalk on the chalkboard. I was hoping that maybe I had the wrong classroom, I was not feeling this class.

I could not help but turn and look at Dan behind me. I smiled at him. He gave me a little smile and whispered "Hello." and nodded his head. I heard "I see that being late is not the only thing you are good at." "Disrupting the class can be added to the list of things you need to improve on." I quickly turned around as I felt the heat rise in my face, everybody in the class was looking at me. Embarrassed I looked down at my desk hoping that would take the attention off me. Mrs. Galant picked up a pile of papers and started walking around the room handing out a coarse outline to every student while she explained what due next class. "There is a short story on my desk, please go and get the assignment and complete an essay for next class." I went up and got the story and sat down and began to read it. Finally, the bell rang, and I quickly left to go to my next class. Dan said, "I will call you later to set up a time for Thursday." As I walked out the door I turned and smiled.

I found my locker quickly and grabbed my binder for Social. I peeked around to see if my friends from junior high were lurking in this packed long wide hallway, there was nobody. The high school is a lot bigger than the junior high. I locked my locker and walked to my next class. At the end of the hallway I saw Nancy, and Patricia. Nancy asked "What class do you have. "I said "Social." She said "So do I." I looked at Patricia and she said disappointedly "I have Science." I said, "Too bad." "We can meet after class if you would like to go to the mall for lunch?" She smiled and said "Yes." Nancy and I found our class and sat down beside each other.

The teacher stood up from his desk, walked over to the door and said, "This is a great looking group of people," closed the door and said, "Good morning, my name is Mr. Scott." As he rocked back and forth on his feet, his hands in his pockets, he had an English accent. "I am here to help you succeed; I will provide you the material on the exams so you will not have to read a lot of material out of class." I turned and looked at Nancy and she smiled at me. Yes, easy class I thought to myself. Mr. Scott said, "In class you will be taking notes and memorizing them for the exam." My smile got even bigger. Mr. Scott took his hands out of his pockets and he turned and went to the chalk board and started writing, he looked over his shoulder and said, "I know that I don't have to tell you all to take notes." And went back to writing. We spent the whole class taking notes.

The bell rang, I closed my binder and left with Nancy to go meet Patricia. When I got to my locker, I noticed that the locker beside me was taken, oh well I thought to myself. Just then Patricia walked up to the locker beside me and started to turn the combination. I laughed and said "Really?" she smiled and said "Yeah." Nancy came up behind Patricia and put her binder in the locker and asked, "Do you want to get lunch?" Happily, I exclaimed, "Yeah, you bet." We closed our lockers and walked out the doors to the mall. As we were walking to the mall I turned and looked at them and said, "I am glad we met." They smiled and said, "Me too." I really liked my new friends.

We walked into the food court like we owned it. We walked right up to Cockney Kids and ordered fries and gravy. We found a table available closest to Cockney Kids and sat down to enjoy our lunch, endless amount of people came over to say hi to Patricia and Nancy that I did not know. I finished up my fries and said, "I have to pick up a few things for mom, I will meet you at school." they smiled and said, "See you later." I walked into Woolco, with what was left of the twenty dollars Dan gave me I got some coffee and cigarettes for mom. The cashier handed me the change, I put it in my pocket and went back to school.

The new school year was winding down, and the people were starting to look familiar. We stood there smiling at everybody as we waited for the bus. The bus pulled up and Patricia discreetly pushed her way up to the front, Nancy and I followed. Patricia had such a calm sweetness to her that I would have let her in front of me. We quickly made our way back on the bus and sat down. The bus made its way to the Bus Terminal and filled just as quickly. Once there we piled off and waited for the bus to take us home.

I lit up a cigarette and was smoking just outside the shelter, a bus pulled up and everybody hopped off, at the end of the line was a dark blonde, browned eyed girl with a beautiful smile and white teeth, behind her was a tall brunette whose blue eyes were like a warm clear summers day. They stopped immediately and started talking to Nancy and Patricia. Nancy interrupted what they were saying and introduced me to them. Bailey, Paige this is Autumn." Paige was smiling and said "Hi." her eyes looked glossy. Bailey smiled and said "Hi." and they continued talking to Nancy and Patricia. Bailey would start a sentence and Paige would finish it with enthusiasm.

Nancy took a drag of her cigarette and put it out. Bailey said, "School sucks, I hate it, so lame." "What a bunch of losers." Paige said." "Seriously, Like Oh My God!" I could not keep up to what they were saying. They were still in Grade eight and nine, that made them thirteen and fourteen years old. I was drawn to them. I found the girls remarkably interesting, their big high hair, baggy pants, and Adidas sweaters over their turtlenecks. I thought that would hide my maturing body, I did not see that in junior high. Our bus came and they said "Hey, see you around." Nancy and Patricia said, "Yes for sure, we will see you around." I said, "It was nice to meet you." We quickly walked over to the bus stop and got on the bus.

Nancy and Patricia chatted while I looked around the bus at all the people, they were so interesting. I had a short bus ride and before I knew it, I was saying "See you tomorrow." I quickly walked home knowing exactly what I was in for, I was prepared today though. I got in the house and mom was sitting with her legs crossed on top of the table. She said, "Autumn did you get me some smokes?" I looked down as I took my shoes off. I said "Yes, and some coffee." I put the cigarettes on the table and the coffee in the cupboard and walked into the living room and turned the TV on to watch Much Music.

I was just getting into watching TV and mom said, "Autumn make me coffee." I sighed and got up and made her a coffee I placed it on the table. She did not say anything, did not even look at me. I went into the kitchen and put some bread in the toaster I asked mom "Would you like some toast?" She said "Yah, OK." I buttered her toast and took it to her, and put peanut butter and Jam on mine, poured a glass of milk and sat down in the living room and finished watching Much Music. I turned the TV off and went upstairs, changed my clothes, grabbed my Walkman went downstairs had a glass of water, and put my runners on and said "I am going for a run. "Then left out the door.

I pushed play on my Walkman and started walking to the pathway, listening to Bon Jovi. Once there I started to run, then did interval training. I was running as fast as I could go, for as long as I could go. I could hear the leaves crackling under foot. This is my time with God. I loved to run; I was running to God. I started singing praise "Jesus, holy spirit, I love you, I need you." Once at the lake I stopped at the bench and started some stretches, I felt so free, so alive, I reached up to the sky and said, "Thank you Lord, I am blessed to be able to run." I bent over to touch the ground with my hands and looked out at the lake and said, "Thank you Lord for my eyes to see the beautiful things that you create."

I started to run around the lake and made my way back to the bench, sat down and closed my eyes. The scent of Fall was in the air, all I could do was breath in and enjoy it. My legs felt like jelly as I stood up, I bolted for as long as I could then slowed down, beads of sweat dripping from my forehead, I took my t - shirt and wiped my face, stepped up onto the stairs of the house going directly upstairs and had a long shower.

Once out of the shower I grabbed the towel off the towel rack. I could not help but take a closer look at my body, my breasts are small but perky, they looked even. Singing, "Thank you, God for my other breast." Touching them they felt the same, my hands moving to touch the stretch marks on my hips, they were small and curvy. Stepping back from the mirror to get a full view I turned and looked over my shoulder to get a look at myself from behind. The tan lines from summer still there but slightly faded.

I wrapped the towel around myself, went into my bedroom and slipped into my favorite pajamas. they were baby blue pants with mint green polka dots, the top matched the blue with no polka dots. They were baggy and hid my maturing body perfectly, I was not yet comfortable with my new additions.

I went downstairs, got a glass of water, and turned around to see if mom moved from the table. She was still sitting there, this time her feet were on a chair, her face had no expression. I drank my water and walked over to give her a kiss. She smelt like cigarette smoke. She moved her head towards me, and I leaned in and kissed her cheek and said, "Good night." "Night." She said not moving, her eyes watched me as I walked up the stairs. I pulled my blankets back, cuddled in and fell asleep.

CHAPTER 6
I Do Not Kiss 'N' Tell

It has been a couple of weeks since school started, everybody is settled in for the school year and the excitement is gone. I have not seen Lisa yet, so when I got off the bus, I told Nancy and Patricia "I will catch up with you later." I walked to the front doors. The main atrium was immediately in the entry, two stories high with windows cut out in the ceiling. Off to the right is a long hallway that led to a few other hallways, one that my locker was in. I started to walk down the hallway, there were windows on one side of the hall. Lined up in front of the windows were about ten black girls with braids, or hair extensions, trendy clothes, and pointy shoes. I felt like I was stepping into a different country where I did not belong. The giggling and laughing stopped as I made my way down the hall, I could feel all eyes on me in silence. I looked down trying not to make eye contact with any of them, I heard one of the girls kiss her teeth and say, "White chic trying to be black." They all started to laugh, and it echoed down the hall. I lifted my head up and pretended they did not bother me. A tall, skinny girl with curly, shoulder length hair and a blonde streak in the front stared me down.

I continued my way out of the hall of judgement to look down the hallways branching off to see if I could see Lisa. Turning down a hallway, walking to the door that led outside. I looked out the window, smiling when I saw Lisa standing outside having a cigarette with her boyfriend Cameron. Lisa was my height, her hair was different, it was styled like Madonna's in the True-Blue video. She had a white jacket on that said Beauty Culture in teal green writing. Cameron was tall, tanned, blonde hair and brown eyes. I opened the door and said "Hi." They smiled and said "Hi" They put out their cigarettes started to make their way to class. Lisa said, "Meet me at the break." she quickly kissed me and left.

I was outside waiting for Lisa and Cameron, Cameron said, "Hey, how's it going?" as they came outside. I smiled and said "Good." Lisa asked, "How is mom?" I smiled and said, "The same." We did not talk about much; it was nice just being with her. I remember the day Lisa left. She was crying because mom had no cigarettes and Lisa could not get any for her, Mom was getting mean, I was scared and did not know what to do. Lisa said, "I am fucking leaving, and I am not coming back." She meant it.

At lunch time when we got to the mall it was busier than usual, we were looking for a table to sit down at but the area we always sat at was full. I heard somebody Say "Nancy." We all turned and looked but I could not see who she was talking to, it was that busy. From the corner of my eye there was a black guy with a red and blue jacket sitting beside the table of the people Nancy and Patricia were talking to. I looked around to decide what I was going to eat, not making up my mind, I tapped Nancy on the shoulder and said, "I will find you in a minute, I am going to the washroom."

Walking out of the washroom I felt a force pull me forward then threw me up against the wall. I felt something across my throat, there was something big and squishy on my lips and then something shoved down my throat. Shocked, I wondered what is going on, what was that? Then the force was released and there was that black guy with his hands on my shoulders. His eyes were big as he said with disbelief "Oh my God! You are still a virgin!" I was frozen, the hallway was dim. Looking at him scared, I did not know what to do, my heart was beating hard, still looking at him with my mouth open, he let go of my shoulders. I Swiftly ran out the mall doors, hearing the door bang behind me, slipping in with the other kids going into school to get away.

I sat in the atrium overcome by astonishment. I did not know what to do. Wondering, did that just happen, did a completely strange black man just stick his tongue down my throat? I did not even know black people were real until the summer before grade seven when I moved from a small northern town in Saskatchewan. I thought they were only on TV. My hands were shaking as I wiped my lips. He almost swallowed my whole face it felt like he has choking me in the process. I have never kissed any boy like that, other than a linger on the lips. The tears were filling my eyes. Overcome with panic I quickly walked to the back doors of the school and through the school yard. The tears were streaming down my face. I gained my composure, walked to the bus stop, and waited for the bus to take me to the Bus Terminal.

I got off the bus and walked across the street to the mall. I looked around for a while, with the few dollars I had left from the money Dan gave me I bought a pack of cigarettes for mom and headed back to the Bus Terminal. The bus from school was pulling up, I sat there waiting for Nancy and Patricia to get off the bus. Not paying attention to the people in front of them getting off, finally they appeared saying, "Hey, where were you?" I said, "I had a doctor's appointment." Bailey and Paige came from the opposite direction, the chatting and giggling started, helping me forget what had happened as we crossed over to the mall. I was surprised by how many people they knew.

Bailey and Paige talked a lot, Baileys favorite thing to say is, "It sucks." Paige likes to say, "No doubt." They were like a married couple, they hated school and everybody. Bailey said, "We are going to your school tomorrow, we will meet you at mall for lunch." Bailey handed Nancy her phone number and said, "Call me later, I have to go home now." We all walked back to the bus terminal and headed home.

Bailey and Paige were at the mall for lunch like they said they would be, they walked with us back to school. As we approached the cross walk, I looked on the other side of the street and that black guy from yesterday was standing there watching us. I slowed down and fell behind everybody hoping to pass by without him noticing. Drawing closer to the other side of the street, my heart was beating fast and I was shaking, everybody started to say hello to him, I kept walking, right past him into the school, directly to the bathroom, to the last stall. Making sure the door was locked, I sat on the back of the toilet, putting my feet on the seat, I stayed there for a while and cried, I did not care about being late for class because I did not know what to do.

On the bus ride home Nancy, Patricia, Bailey, and Paige were saying how cute Cody was. I sat there, unable to say anything. Then Patricia looked at me and said, "Cody was asking about you." I sat there silently looking at Patricia, I felt paralyzed. They all giggled and started talking about Cody again. I faked a smile, the events of yesterday played through my mind, when he pinned me against the wall and kissed me. I thought to myself that I would like to never see him again.

That night I laid in bed tossing and turning, I could not sleep, finally saying, "You are being silly, he is just asking about you, just ignore him, he'll go away." "Yeah that's it, that is what I will do." I took a deep breath in and exhaled, praying, "God I love you, you are my father, please protect me." Not giving Cody another thought.

The next day I was tired. I sat in the food court talking to Nancy, Patricia, Bailey, and Paige when I heard somebody whisper in my right ear, "Hello." I turned around and looked, Cody was standing there smiling. Being caught off guard nervously I said "Hi." Cody said, "I don't believe that we officially met, I am Cody." Cody looked at Nancy and asked, "Do you mind if I join you?" Nancy smirked and nodded. Cody sat down, I blushed, saying, "I have to do something for my mom, I will meet you at school." They nodded, I got up and said, "Excuse me." As I was walking through Woolco and was startled, I felt somebody grab my arm. It was Cody. He pulled me towards him and whispered, "I will be alone with you one day." He let go of my arm and smiled at me. I turned around on my heels and thought to myself, I do not think so, yuck. I quickly started to walk through the store towards school, glancing back, Cody keep walking like nothing just happened.

I told mom I was not feeling well so I could stay home for the rest of the week. Nancy lent me a book by V.C Andrews Called Flowers in The Attic, for two days I stayed in bed and read. I only got up to Shower and eat. Nancy called on Friday evening after supper to see how I was. I said, "I haven't been feeling well, I am fighting a cold." Nancy said "Oh, well I hope you feel better." "What are you doing this weekend?" I told her "I am working on Saturday, and Sunday, but I will see you on Monday." She said "Ok, see you Monday." She hung up the phone. I could not help my mind wondering back to Cody when he grabbed my arm and what he said. I wanted to tell her that Cody was creeping me out, and what he did. My virginity is a gift for my husband. Asking God, "How did Cody know I am a virgin, is it that obvious?"

Dan came in to see me at work on Sunday because he missed me at school. I just told him "I wasn't feeling well but feel good now." We sat there and talked for a while and then his mom's boyfriend Peter came in. He stood about six feet tall, in his late fifties, early sixties. Always wore a tennis shirt and jeans that did not fit his waist, so they hung below his belly, grey thinning hair with blue eyes, and was missing most of his teeth on the bottom of his mouth. He handed me eighty dollars and said, "You can go now, I am closing up. I will see you next weekend." I smiled and said, "Thank you." Dan said, "I will catch the bus with you because this area is scary, and I don't want anything to happen to you."

It was a scary area, it was in the core of downtown, the prostitutes hang out on the corner all time. The buildings were all run down and graffitied, on the inside and outside, with broken windows. The sidewalks had cut up pop bottles, discarded needles after being shared among everybody. I said to Dan "I recognize some of the people from the store but not everybody." He replied, "Just because you recognize them doesn't mean that you can trust them." "They are addicts, they drink Lysol and use needles." Dan looked at me and said in a stern voice, and deep concern in his eyes, "You have to be careful." I smiled at Dan and said "Ok, I will."

I got home, and before I could take my shoes off mom asked me with a distressed voice, "Do you have any cigarettes? "I quickly said "No, I will get you some, do you want anything else?" She quickly said "Pepsi." I walked through the house and out the back door to the small green space that separated the back of the store from our house. Alongside of the building I saw Marty walking towards home. Marty is two years older than me. His parents owned the hair salon right next to the Convenience Store. Marty's hair looked like Bon Jovi, He was wearing a teal blue plaid dress shirt with a leather tie and jeans. He smiled and said," Hi Autumn". I could not help but have a big smile. I said "Hello." Marty said, "Dad forgot his wallet and cigarettes at the Salon, so I was just grabbing them for him." I said, "I am going to the store you want to join me?" He said "Sure." As we walked home, we talked about normal teenager stuff, he asked about Lisa. Since Lisa started to date Cameron, he does not hear from her. I affirmed the same thing. Mike said, "It was nice seeing you, talk to you later." I said, "You too." We both disappeared in the house. I flipped off my shoes and gave mom the Pepsi and cigarettes. She said, "I will be so glad when the cheque comes in." Going up the stairs I said, "Yeah that will be nice."

The next morning as our bus pulled up to the bus terminal, Patricia waved to Bailey and Paige as they stood outside of the crowded shelter. Patricia exclaimed "Hey there's Cody!" She waved. I was taken back, my eyes got big and I looked out the window. I felt a little scared, my legs were shaking. I have never seen him at the bus terminal. Cody was standing there talking to

Bailey and Paige. It was the first time that I got a full view of him. His hair was curly just above his shoulders, His teeth were white and perfectly straight, about five feet ten inches tall, it looked like he probably worked out. He had a broad chest compared to all the other kids. He was wearing the same blue and red jacket, with a pair of blue loose-fitting Levi's five o one button fly jeans and black dress shoes. I realized I was the last one off the bus, so I quickly got off and walked over where girls were and stood back.

Patricia asked, "What are you doing here Cody?" Cody replied, "I am going to see a friend, we are going to play video games." The conversation changed. I saw the bus coming so I walked over to the bus stop and everybody started to line up. I sat near the back of the bus in the seat where I could see into the aisle, Patricia and Nancy sat down on each side of me. Cody sat right across from me and Paige and Bailey sat on either side of him. He was staring directly at me smiling. I turned my head and looked the window in front of us and tried not to look at him. Patricia asked, "How old are you?" Cody replied "Eighteen." Patricia kept asking questions about him. I felt anxious the whole bus ride and tried not to look at Cody. I would occasionally give the girls a smile and hoped that they would not see my fear. Finally, the bus pulled up to the school, everybody but me waved and said "Bye." I took a deep breath in and locked my gaze in the direction I was going, Cody stayed on the bus.

As we walked to the smoking area just outside the doors to have a cigarette, Nancy and Patricia grabbed my arms on either side and started to giggle. They said, "I think Cody really likes you, he is eighteen." "He is really hot!" "Do you like him?" I strongly blurted out "No, No I don't like him. My mind was screaming, I am a virgin, he does not like me, he just wants my virginity. Biting my lip to stop myself from telling them why he was showing up, and that I was scared. I did not know them that well, they may not believe me. Their facial expressions were shocked, they looked at each other, I changed the subject and asked Bailey and Paige "why are you not at school, what do you do?" Bailey said, "Hang Out, not much." Paige laughed and said, "pretty much" I said, "I am going to class, see you later." They stood there a little confused.

We were walking through the food court and I heard what I thought to be Mom calling "Autumn." I turned and looked and saw Mom sitting with Lisa, Mom waved and said "Hi, hi." I looked at Nancy and Patricia and said, "I will find you in a minute." They nodded, I sat down. Mom only went out when she had money, she got her cheque. Mom asked, "Do you want some money to get a bite to eat?" I said, "No thanks, I have money." It was nice to see Lisa and Mom together, I missed that. I said, "I am going to go get some fries." Mom said, "That sounds good get me some too, oh and gravy."

Walking back to the table I saw that Cody and a couple other boys sitting with the girls. One boy was Chinese, the other boy was white with brown hair. both had shoulder length hair with Jerry curls. The white boy wore his ball cap backwards. I went the long way back and sat down with Lisa and Mom instead of with them. I looked at the clock and still had ten minutes. I asked Lisa "When are you going back to school?" Lisa said, "I am going to stay here for a while." I asked, "Do you want to go look in some stores quickly before I go back to school?" A smile went across mom's face, she nodded her head yes and said, "Yeah, Ok sure."

We got up and walked into the main part of the mall and blended in with the crowd. We had to walk a little bit slower because mom could not walk that fast. Mom would stop and look at clothes and when she saw something, she liked she say, "Oh look at that." see the price tag and keep walking. "When I get some money, I am going to go shopping." She was so childlike in a lot of ways. While Mom was looking, I kept looking around to see if I could see Cody. We got on the escalator to take us downstairs, I kept looking up to the top, hoping Cody was not lurking around. Mom was looking at the stores below and said, "Oh let's go look in there, oh then in there." We got to the bottom of the escalator and I said "Mom, I am going back to school." She replied "Ok." I kissed her cheek and said, "I love you, bye Lisa." She said "Bye, see you later." Feeling nervous, I hustled up the escalator in Woolco, accelerated through the parking lot, dodging in and out between vehicles in hopes that I will not be noticed.

I was so distracted in English class wondering, how do I handle this difficult situation? Covering my face with my hands, running my fingers through my hair, resting my hands on my shoulders, giving them a massage. I asked myself, do I have this right to feel this way? I felt a poke on the back of my right shoulder. I turned around and Dan asked, "Are you ok?" Shaking, I stammered, "Yeah, will you get the homework for me, I am going to go home." Dan said, "Are you sure?" I said "Yeah" Not sure I convinced him of, but he said "Ok, not a problem."

I picked up my things, walked up to the front of the class to Mrs. Galant's desk where she was sitting, pleading, hoping she would have mercy, "Mrs. Galant, I am not feeling well, I need to go home." She lifted her head just enough to see her eyebrows raised, looking at me over glasses when she said, in a voice just loud enough for everybody to hear, "Is that right? Fine, just know that if you leave you won't be coming back to this class." I glanced around the room and saw that everybody in the classroom was staring at me. I looked at her making eye contact, firmly saying, "Fine." I flipped my hair back, my glare challenging her as I walked out of the classroom.

I waited for Nancy and Patricia between classes outside where we always met. They both came outside, Nancy had a bounce in her step and her head bobbed, saying "Hello." Patricia had a great big smile on her face, she lifted her shoulders a little and said "Hi." Nancy asked, "Who were you with at lunch?" I said, "That's my mom and sister." "My sister goes to school here, but I never see her because she has a boyfriend." I kind of giggled out loud. I smiled and said, "I am going to go home now, but I will see tomorrow." Nancy put her cigarette in the canister they both said, "OK, see you tomorrow." They did not ask about mom and her disability and it made me feel good, I did not offer any information.

When I got home Lisa and Mom were sitting at the kitchen table talking. Lisa said "Hi, guess what, mom bought us some clothes for picture day tomorrow." I said "Oh?" there were a couple of bags on the table, Lisa pulled out a red and a black sweater and two pairs of black pants. She handed me the red sweater and a pair of pants saying, "Try it on!" I quickly put the pants on and pulled the sweater over my head. the pants fit perfectly, snug where needed, and loose where I like it to be loose. The red sweater was turtleneck, did not look the best, just not my color. I went downstairs to show them, and my mom looked happy. I said to Lisa "Let me see you!" Lisa came out of the washroom, she looked beautiful. Her naturally platinum blonde hair went with everything. There is not a color she did not look good in. Even though I already knew the answer I asked, "Can I try the black sweater?" Lisa said "No, this is mine." I bleached my hair and it did not matter how much I do it, there is always red trying to burst through like a fire. I sighed thinking red is not my color.

When I got on the bus the next day, both Nancy and Patricia noticed that I had a new outfit on. It was obvious when you wear the same thing every day. Nancy said, "Is that a new outfit?" I said "Yeah." I was wearing it proudly, at least the pants, but I did not want to hurt my Mom's feelings. Nancy and Patricia both smiled and said, "It looks nice." I said, "Thank you." and sat down, hoping that they would not notice my sister plucked most of my eyebrows out last night, just in time for pictures.

Lunch was great, no interruptions, Cody was not there, or his friends. It was just Nancy, Patricia, Bailey, and Paige. we talked, we laughed, and enjoyed the new friendships that we have formed. I felt so wonderful and free from my worries. Bailey and Patricia walked us back to school, as we approached the crosswalk Paige said "Hey! Isn't that Cody?" "Are those flowers for you Autumn?" It was hard not to focus on Cody, the flowers were huge! Bright red roses, they were beautiful. As we approached, I could see baby's breath peeking from the bunch. We stepped onto the curb, Cody stepped forward and said with a smile "Autumn, these are for you." The aroma of the roses lingered under my nose, I stepped back a bit and did not know what to say, I was speechless. Cody said, "When somebody gives you flowers you take them." I did not want Cody to get any ideals I said, "I will not take those, I am sorry." Everybody was watching Cody moved towards me and gently pulled me towards him and saying, "Take the flowers, everybody is watching, you do not want to disappoint them." I silently took the flowers. Cody whispered in my ear, "We will be alone one day!" As he let go of me, he pushed me just enough for me to get the hint. His dark eyes hollow. Deep down inside I knew what he meant. Embarrassed I stepped back and just stared at the roses.

Paige blurted, "You are so lucky Autumn, Cody really likes you and he bought you flowers!" "I wish I had somebody to buy me flowers." I looked at Paige and gave a half smile, I did not say anything. I quickly walked to my locker and put the roses inside and locked the door, after school I threw them in the dumpster beside my house, saying, "Nobody will know. For the rest of the week Cody was on our bus in the morning sitting closer and closer. He was at the mall for lunch and caught the bus to the Bus Terminal. The two boys from the food court, Dakota, and Luc showed up a couple of times. I was thankful the weekend was here, not having the pressure of Cody, was very relieving.

I went to work on Saturday and Sunday as usual and Dan came by to keep me company on Saturday. The Youth Group had a birthday party for one of the girls, so he did not come Sunday. It was a busy weekend because the welfare cheques were out. Peter was in to make sure nothing would happen to me. The day went by quickly. Peter locked up the door and we balance the till. I was sitting on a stool with my legs crossed, waiting for him to say it was good. Peter looked at me and asked, "How old are you again?" I said "Fifteen." Not taking his eyes off me he said, "I know that you haven't been with a man before." I blushed and thought, how inappropriate, is it that obvious? Peter moved towards me saying, "I will give you one thousand dollars to give it to me." I was shocked, firmly saying "No, I have to go before it starts to get dark." Peter reached in front of me and opened the cash register, I looked down and noticed a cockroach hop from the cord to the register onto my shoe and scuffled down the side of the counter.

Peter handed me one hundred dollars and said, "Think about it." I quickly hopped off the stool and left.

I laid in bed for a while, not able to sleep. I most certainly did not want to go to school tomorrow and I did not think that going back to work was a good idea either. I needed to make some money to help my mom pay bills. I murmured, "What am I going to do?" I tossed and turned all night and before I knew it, my alarm went off and it was time to get up. I cried out loud "Why God?"

As we pulled into the bus terminal Cody, was there with Paige, and Bailey. We got off the bus and they were talking about how they met up over the weekend at the mall and hung out. Bailey looked at me and said, "You should have been there it was fun." I smiled and said happily "I had to work." We all got on the bus to go to school, and when we got off, I was looking for an excuse to leave, "I am going to go find Lisa." I blurted and left. I walked through the school, out the back doors, and hopped on a bus, enjoying the bus ride home.

I missed a few days of school, Nancy and Patricia were concerned but glad to see me. Thankfully, Cody was not at the bus terminal, but as we pulled up to the school, Cody was however standing there waiting, I tried to walk past him, he stepped in front of me, saying with a smile, loud enough for everyone to hear, "Where have you been?" "We are all worried about you." He grabbed me and pulled me into him giving me a hug. He whispered, "You belong to me, do you understand?" "You are mine." I pushed away from him and said, "No way, never."

I turned around leading with my head walking into the school to find Lisa. She was upstairs by her locker getting her books for class, she looked beautiful as always. I walked over and gave her a hug saying, "I love you Sissy." The feelings were returned but, quickly interrupted when we heard, "There you are!" "I have been looking all over for you." Cody came down the hall and grabbed my arm. Lisa grabbed my other arm and said, "Who in the hell are you?" He said, "I am a friend and I am making sure that Autumn gets to class, she has been skipping." He started to pull me. Lisa pulled me towards her and said, "I am her sister and I will make sure she gets to class." Cody let go and left. Lisa looked at me and asked, "Who is that?" I said "Nobody." Quickly changing the subject, I asked Lisa, "Do you want to skip class and go to the mall to hang out?" I smiled "I have money." Lisa smiled and said "Sure just let me tell Cameron so he knows where I am."

When I got home mom said, "Amy called from one of the places you applied at called, the number is right there," Then pushed the piece of paper towards me. I grabbed the phone and dialed the number, running upstairs, returning with a big smile on my face. My mom asked, "What did she want?" I jumped up and squealed, "I have an interview," I turned around excited. She asked "When?" I squealed "Tomorrow." Mom Said "Oh, good." The stress was overwhelming, it was hard enough that I had to work while in school, the last thing I needed was someone like Cody in my life. I swallowed my pride, apologizing to Mrs. Galant so she would let me back into English class. However, she never did like me, nothing changed, she had her favorite and it was not me.

Walking through the door after school, there were a pair of men's shoes in the doorway. I stood behind the railing going upstairs, I looked over at the kitchen table and froze. Cody was sitting at the table talking to my mom. I did not know what to say, I stood there, finally finding the words, "What are you doing here?" He said, "I am talking to your mom." I was telling your mom how I have no place to live. Your mom said that I could live here. Looking at mom with fear in my eyes. She started to giggle, looking at Cody when she said, " you black son of a bitch, you better keep your pecker in your pants, or I will hang you from the ceiling by your black balls." Laughing, I was not sure if it was an evil laugh, or a little girl's laugh.

Shocked, I ran out the door to the park, climbing the ladder to the tree house, and I was shaking, I was overtaken by the smell of urine. Looking around it was a small space, about four by four. I crawled to the entryway and looked outside to make sure Cody did not follow me. Crawling back into the corner I hugged my legs. At least it is covered and blocking the wind. Nighttime was getting cold outside. Trying to process what just happened. All I could think was what is she thinking? I looked up and asked, "How does Cody know where I live?" I have nowhere to go. My oldest brother is in the army, I have no idea where my other brother is, Lisa made it quite clear the last time I crashed on her couch that it I was only welcome for a couple of nights. Before I realized it, my pants were wet from my tears. I wiped my face; I was horrified and alone. I said, "I can't leave her." Why would mom let a stranger in our home?"

It was hours before I made my way back to the house, it was going down below zero at night, the air is smelling like snow. The lights were off, quietly I opened the unlocked door, and started to tiptoe up the stairs, going to the bathroom and got ready for bed. Moving as quietly as I could to my bedroom, slipping under the covers. I was so emotionally drained that my head hit the pillow and I fell asleep.

I woke up the next morning to Cody sitting on the edge of my bed, his hand on my left hip, my back to him. He gently caressed my hip and I jolted awake and moved to the opposite side of the bed, pulling my blankets up only revealing my neck. Cody said, "Good Morning." I did not answer him. He said, "I guess you are not a morning person." Unsure of what to expect, I stood up on the bed and tried to jump off, he reached out and quickly grabbed me by my pajama pants, pulling them down just enough to catch a glimpse of my underwear, He then gave another yank and pulled me down to the bed. He said, "Those are nice flowers on your underwear, can't wait to see the rest of them." Pinning me down, he started kissing me.

I started to kick and fight, anything to try and get away, my strength was not enough to get him off me. I started to scream, and he sat on top of me and quickly covered my mouth with both of his hands. He said, "Stop screaming and I will get off of you." "OK?" I nodded my head he slowly took his hands off my mouth and then got off me. I moved as fast as I could, away from him. grabbing my clothes, running to the bathroom to change.

Cody closed the door before I could get out, asking, "Where are you going?" I said, "To change, so I can get away from you." Cody smiled saying, "You don't have to leave to change, I want to see what belongs to me, you are mine." Clinging to my clothes I said, "Let me out or I will start screaming." Cody smiled, confidently saying, "I guess we have some time." He opened the door and I squeezed past him through the doorway keeping my eyes on him the whole time.

After changing I made my way back to my bedroom, Cody was sat there watching me put my mascara on. I turned and looked at him asking, "Do you mind?" He said, "Not at All." I closed the lid and put it in my pocket, I grabbed my sweater and went downstairs, putting my shoes on. Cody stayed hot on my trail, not giving me room to breathe.

Walking out the door, Cody was right beside me, reaching out he grabbed my arm, pulled me so I was facing him, moving an inch away from my face, firmly saying, " I told you that you are mine, we will be alone together and that is what I want, I always get what I want. You, will not go anywhere, and I am not there, Understand." He let go of my arm and I looked at him retorting, "Never." Turning to walk away. He grabbed my arm again, pulled me closer saying, "I get what I want, you know what I want." grabbing my head, roughly kissing me, finally releasing his lips, smacking my bottom as he smiled. I could feel the heat rising in my face as I blushed. Embarrassed I quickly turned away and kept walking. Cody said, "Are you blushing? Oh my God you are blushing, I cannot believe this."

Nancy and Patricia were surprised to see Cody get on the bus with me. Cody said with a smile from ear to ear "I wanted to talk to Autumn." I sat beside Nancy and faced Patricia, Cody sat down beside Patricia and faced me. I could not make eye contact with Cody; the smile did not leave his face. Patricia asked, "Why are you so happy?" Cody happily said, "I am happy, my talk with Autumn went well." I was surprised how Cody played this charming person with them after what he just did, he was different, just like that.

Nancy and I were practicing the fish tail, and French braids on each other in beaty culture, I asked, "Can I have a sleepover at your house tonight?" "It is a school night." Nancy replied, I smiling I said, "We can go to school together in the morning." She gave a slight nod saying, "Sure." "Maybe Patricia can come too?" I mischievously said. "Yeah, we can do that." Nancy said convinced. The bus came to my stop, Cody got up to get off the bus, I stayed behind, Cody looked at me saying, "This is our stop, are you coming?" "No, I am going to Nancy's." I said without wincing. Cody smiled when he said, "See you guys later." and got off the bus. I knew he was mad, did not show it though, I had the feeling of self-satisfaction; Cody will know that I have no interest in being with him.

The bus went by Patricia's place, then went a little further, Nancy rung the bell for the next stop, we got off in front of a green space and crossed the street. The houses were newer, and big, I did not pay attention to the directions to Nancy's because I was too busy looking at the beautiful houses. When we got to Nancy's the smell of cooking lingered in the air. I asked, "What is that smell?" "It smells wonderful." Nancy replied, "Shepherd's Pie." We went directly upstairs to Nancy's room. It was beautiful, it looked like it was out of a magazine. I looked out her window into the backyard and said, "Dude, you have a swimming pool?" Patricia walked over to the window. Nancy smiled and said "Yup, it is closed up for the winter."

I flopped down on Nancy's bed, the pink and white floral comforter was fluffy, sinking into the bed, thinking, mmm, I can go to sleep right now. It was so cozy. After we ate supper, we walked over to the convenience store to get Slurpee's. we talked well into the night, somehow all three of us fit on Nancy's single bed and managed to sleep comfortably.

CHAPTER 7
Sweet Sixteen

In the morning we all got up, got ready for school, and caught bus together. Cody was not around until lunch, we sat at the usual table when suddenly, I felt a yank on the back of my jacket, it almost pulled me off my seat. Looking behind me, Cody was standing there. He looked around the table, smiled saying, "Sorry I didn't mean to do that, I need to talk to you." I replied "No, I have nothing to say." Cody gently pulled me and guided me out of my seat saying, "This will only take a second. "He put his arm around me and led me just outside the doors of the mall.

He leaned against me pinning me up against the wall, his arm across my chest, angrily he said "You think you can pull that shit; you don't know who you are dealing with." His eyes contacted mine, as he continued, "I always get what I want, you are mine, do you hear me?" Not answering, I turned my head, he followed to get a better look, intrigued he said, "Wow, you have two different colored eyes." He kissed my lips and let go of me. He turned and walked to the doors, pulled it open firmly saying, "Let's go."

I sat down at the table, Cody sat in the chair beside me, grabbing my knee and squeezing it. I turned my head so he would not see my face, trying to brush his hand off my knee, but his grip was too tight. All I could think was why is happening, why won't he leave me alone? I am freaking out right now, I do not know what to do. Cody leaned over and whispered in my ear, "Tonight is the night." I sighed saying, "I work tonight."

I thanked God when I got my period at work, when I got home, I went into the bathroom to put a pad on, there was a tampon there, it was a regular size, picking it up and I held it in my hand, staring at it as I slid down the wall, my bottom hitting the floor. I felt my eyes tear up, pleading, "God, I want to be a virgin on my wedding night." I slipped the tampon back in the drawer, looking at myself in the mirror saying, "Don't give up faith, God please, I want to be a virgin." I Flipped the light switch off and went downstairs.

Cody and Dakota came into the house when I was watching TV, Dakota's older brother Jamie was in my grade eight science class. Tall, dark hair, brown eyes. He paid attention in class and was quiet, he seemed smart. Dakota was so much shorter and always dressed like a gangster, opposite from Jamie. They sat down on either side of me, Cody started to whisper in my ear "Tonight is the night." Dakota laughed and started to sing Naughty by Nature, O.P.P. He jumped up and started to dance while he sang, "You down with OPP yeah you know me." I pretended to ignore him because I did not listen to gangster rap, but they are always playing Too Short, Boogie down productions, and NWA.

I stormed to go upstairs, Cody followed me and grabbed my arm when I stormed upstairs, firmly saying, "It is happening tonight." I yanked my arm away, saying proudly like I won the war, "I have my period." Turning, I continued up the stairs, to my room, falling asleep.

Cody had some friends over; mom was getting high with them. I was starting to feel like I was the adult, mom was the child, but less experienced. I walked past my mom in the kitchen and I went upstairs to change into my workout clothes to go for a run, grabbing my Walkman, put on my runners, and left. I was gone for a long time, it felt like hours. I love running, no cares in the world. I have always been a long-distance runner; it just came naturally, and I was good at it. Coming up to the house and I could hear the music playing, the smell of pot and hash was in the air, you could get high off the fumes, I opened the door, there were a few more people there then when I left. I rolled my eyes on my way upstairs for a shower.

I slipped into my pajamas and went downstairs to get some water, I could hear my mom laughing and saying to Cody, "You are fucking crazy, here pass me that fucking joint." I could hear in the background Too Short, don't fight the feeling. Storming over to the stereo, I turned it off affirming, "Party is over, I am going to bed, I have school tomorrow." Cody got up and walked over to me and started to grind up against me, I could feel his body parts rubbing up against mine. "Chill out baby, tonight is the night." He said. I pushed him away and said, "I don't think so, I have my period." Cody grabbed the front of my pajamas and underwear, He pulled them out so he could get a look. Cody let go and the waistband snapped back, he pushed me up against the counter and started to thrust this pelvis towards me repeatedly. he stepped back saying, "Not tonight." He gently guided me to the stairs, placed his hand on bottom, slid it around and grabbed my breasts. Stepping back, I gasped embarrassed. Cody looked at me saying, "It is ok baby, go to bed." There was an audience watching, they were chanting Cody, Cody, Cody.

Flying up the stairs to my room feeling flushed, throwing myself onto my bed. They did not turn the music back on and I would not dare to go back downstairs. I sat there for a while thinking about how the house was chaos before when my family was here, what I would not do for that chaos right now, at least I knew what to expect. I felt so dirty and ashamed, Cody did not care about me, how could he do this? Something I feel so strongly about he just wanted to take it. Why would he cause me so much grief? Why would mom allow this? She saw the whole thing; she knows I am waiting for marriage.

Quietly I said, "God, If I am not giving then he is not taking." Repeating, "If I am not giving, he is not taking." Jumping up quickly, running to the bathroom I locked the door, I pulled open the draw, pulled out the tampon and stared at it as I held it in my hand, looking at myself in the mirror confirming, "God, If I'm not giving, he is not taking." If my husband will not have it, neither will he, God, I give it to you, may your will be done." I turned the shower on to the hotter side and waited for it to get warm. Unwrapping the tampon, holding it in my hand, studying it while I sat on the side of the bathtub. Recalling my youth leader telling me, not to use a tampon because it could take your virginity, that is a gift for one, your husband. Proof that have waited, pledging your love until death. Looking up saying, "God, If I am not giving then he is not taking." My pajamas dropped to the floor, I stepped into the hot shower and put the tampon on the self. The tears started to roll down my face and were quickly washed away by the water, occasionally coming out for breath. I was crying hysterically running my hands through my hair, this was not what I imagined it was going to be like. I quickly grabbed the tampon from the shelf and got a feel for how it works. I opened my thighs just enough to insert the tampon, crying the whole time. The crying stopped and was quickly replaced. Ouch, ouch, ouch, ouch, ouch," I couldn't take it anymore and I pulled the tampon out and started to cry again.

Suddenly I heard a knock on the bathroom door, it was Cody he asked, "What are you doing?" I responded, "I bled through my clothes, so I am having a shower." It grew silent. I turned the shower off and flushed the evidence down the toilet and wiped my tears from eyes. I grabbed my pajama pants and put them on. I looked in the mirror my eyes were red. I looked at my breasts and quickly pulled my top over my head and opened the door and went to bed. My eyes grew heavy and I could not keep them open any longer, I fell asleep.

Surprised to come home from school and Cody was sitting at the table with my Mom. He was never here before me? I went into the kitchen to make spaghetti; Cody came up behind and caress my neck. I rolled my eyes and looked at mom to see if my mom was seeing this, I noticed that she was watching through the corner of her eye. Cody whispered, "Tonight is the night, I cannot wait." I was not understanding, this is my mom, she is supposed to protect me, why isn't she? I turned quickly and looked at him making eye contact, clearly stating, "No." He did say anything, just smiled. I stormed and went an inch from Mom's face asking, "Are you seeing this? What is wrong with you?" She turned and looked at me and said, "What, I am not doing nothing wrong." I looked in her eyes and said, "You are doing nothing." She laughed and said, "What are you talking about, Autumn?" I was so mad;

the doorbell rang so I opened the door. It was Dakota, he looked stoned as usual. "Cody is in the kitchen." I snapped.

I sat in the living room eating my spaghetti, Dakota started to sing, then he started saying mom's name, "Francis, Francis." His voice was high, like out of a horror movie. Cody and Dakota started to laugh. I shouted, "Shut up." Dakota started to say in a taunting high-pitched voice, "Francis, Francis." I got up, Cody pulled me back down, throwing his leg across me saying, "Tonight is the night, baby." Dakota looked at me with a devilish look and laughed. Repeating myself, "No, it's not." Pushing his leg off, "I am going for a run so get your leg off me."

The run relieved some stress that I have been feeling, the shower relaxed my tired muscles, the clean, comfy pajamas were the just the final ingredient for an amazing sleep. Sipping my water, I noticed mom was in bed, the house was quiet, Dakota left. Cody crept into the kitchen, taking my water from my hand, his lips met mine, his tongue slipped down my throat, pushing him away, frustrated I loudly said, "No, stop it." Running up the stairs to sleep with mom, almost at the top, I was stopped, grabbing the railing, Cody started yanking, I could not hold on anymore, He was much stronger than me, I was being pulled down the stairs backwards as I yelled, "NO, no, no!" Practically carrying me Cody forced me down the hallway, opened the basement door, I tried to get away, but could not. Wrestling as Cody, yanked, pulled whatever he could. Listening to him say, "I am taking it right now."

He let go of me and I tried to run. Cody grabbed me and forcefully took off my shirt. He pulled on his pants and the buttons went pop, pop, pop, and his pants fell to the floor and he did not have any underwear on. His penis was erect, I was terrified, it was much bigger than a tampon. He flung me on the bed, I tried to get away, he pulled my pants and underwear off at the same time pinning me down. Cody flipped me on my back I closed my legs, I was screaming "Aahhhh, No, no." He pried my legs apart and wiggled between them, I was screaming "No, no." Cody put his full body weight on top of me and put his hands over my face and said, "SSh!"

His manness between my inner thighs, hands still covering my mouth, my screams were muffled. I must have been screaming louder because he applied more pressure over my mouth and said "Shhh." I could feel him pushing harder and harder, it hurt so bad, until he stopped and lingered. My heart sunk in my chest, I was devastated, Cody said "It's OK." then pulled himself out saying, "I am going to move my hands so be quiet." I could not see him; his hands still covered my face. I nodded. He removed his hands, twisted his body just enough to see that there was no blood. Still on top of me he looked into my eyes, disappointedly saying, "You lied, you aren't a virgin." Cody got off me, I closed my eyes paralyzed. I could feel a tear run down the side of my face. He said, "Why are you crying?" "You fucking lied to me." Cody went upstairs, covering myself up, I lied there for a while, paralyzed, unable to move, I mumbled "It's over." Finally, I rolled over, holding onto the blankets I grabbed my pajamas and got dressed under the covers.

Scared to sleep in my room after that, I slept with mom in her room, thinking I would be safe. The first few nights were peaceful sleeps, I thought I was dreaming when I felt something touching me. Cody grabbed my arm, pulling me out of the bed, half asleep I mumbled, "No." I started to pull back and kept saying "No." Cody pulled harder until we reached my room. He closed the door and placed his hands over my mouth and said, "I am going to make sure that you are not tight for anybody else bitch." I tried to get out, but he grabbed my arm and flung me. I fell to the floor and he picked me up and threw me on the bed. Begging Cody, "Please stop, what do you want?" Cody grabbed my ankle and lifted me up, pulling my pajama pants off. Cody took off his pants and forced himself on me again.

Cody yanked me back down when I got up to go to the washroom asking. "Where do you think you are going?" "To the washroom." I replied, Cody got up and followed me to the bathroom and stood outside the door, making sure I went back to my room instead of sneaking off to mom's room. I was so tired, as I laid there thinking to myself, if this is a nightmare when is it going to end?

Winter was here and it was cold. Cody continued to have his way with me. I could not go anywhere or do anything without him there. I started to skip school a lot with Nancy, Patricia, Bailey, and Paige. We would hang out at the malls and I started to meet lots of people. Cody branded me though, everywhere I went I was referred to as Cody's girl, does Cody know where you are? I could not breathe, I felt trapped.

After hanging out with Nancy and Patricia, Cody frightened me when he came in the house right behind me saying loudly, "There you are, I have been looking all over for you." My eyes started to tear, and I closed them whispering, "Please God help me." Cody grabbed my jacket saying, "I have a surprise for you." He pulled me out the door and was walking so fast and I could barely keep up with him. We got on a bus that I did not normally take, curiously I asked, "Where are you taking me?" He replied, "I am taking you to meet my Mom." "I don't understand." I replied. Cody looked at me and said, "I want my mom to meet you." Cody rung the bell and we got off the bus in front of an apartment, I have seen it before, it was building across from where I worked.

Cody led the way as we walked up the stairs, Cody opened the door and walked right in saying, "Hi Mom." My glance turned to a black lady sitting in a chair by the window. Her feet planted on the floor, her arms resting on the arms of the chair. She looked at Cody but did not say a word. Cody said, "I want you to meet somebody." He sat down on the couch across from her and pulled me down beside him.

Cody said "Mom, this is Autumn, Autumn this is my Mom." She turned her head slightly, looked me up and down and said "Hello." I smiled and said "Hello." It was awkward, nobody really said anything we looked at each other until finally, Cody's Mom asked Cody "Are you working?" The visit ended. Cody got up abruptly and said, "Let's go." I smiled at his mom and said, "It was nice to meet you." She nodded her head and Cody pulled me out the door.

We got on the bus that dropped us off and Cody walked to the back of the bus and sat in the corner. He pulled me down on his lap saying, "You belong to me, you will not go anywhere without everybody knowing that you are mine." "What is that supposed to mean?" I asked confused. Cody responded, "Just what I said, you are mine, you will always be a part of me, and I will always be a part of you." I was on the verge of tears, I did not understand, I am my own person, I belonged to God. Cody lifted me up, putting me on the seat beside him, grabbed my knee, not saying anything else. I crossed my arms and looked out the window trying to figure out what that meant.

Cody pulled a marker out of his pocket, writing Kiss 'n' Cee on the seat. Kiss 'n' Tell was a nickname that I had with my junior high friend Natalia she was Tell and I was Kiss. 'Cee' was Cody's initials, Cody Ethan Erickson. Cody looked at me saying, "See everybody is going to know that you are mine." Kiss was kind of a disguise for me, I have kissed boys before, but it was dangerous, if given the chance they would have had my virginity. I was waiting, only one was worthy of being with me. I was ok with people thinking I kiss a lot of boys, possibly being promiscuous, hoping to deter them from dating me. I knew the truth, most importantly God knew the truth.

The bus pulled up, the girls were standing in the heated terminal, sheltered from the crisp, chilly air. I walked into the terminal and smiled and said "Hi." Nancy looked at me and said "Hey, the community hall is having at dance on Friday night do you want to go?" I asked what happens there? Nancy said, "It's a dance, it happens once a month and it's a lot of fun, it costs ten dollars." I shrugged my shoulders, nodding my head and said "Sure, why not."

Friday could not come soon enough, we were all excited, on the bus home from school, all we could talk about was a dance. Nancy was hoping that Sean was going to be there, never have I met him, I did not know much about him, he was a mystery to me. Paula was hoping Brandon would show up, eyes dreamy, shyly smiling saying, "He so tall, so good looking." Ringing the bell to get off I squealed with excitement, "This is going to be so much fun."

Excitement was building up in me, strategically I brushed each one of my long eye lashes, wanting them to be perfect. "Who are you trying to impress?" Cody blurted. Seeing Cody's reflection in the mirror as his face curled up looking disgusted. "I am just going out with my friends to have fun, I have never been to anything like this before, I like dancing." The phone rang running to pick it up, Nancy was on the other end, she asked, "Do you have any money?" I replied, "I have fifteen dollars, but I need ten to get in the dance." Nancy asked, "Do you want to go in on a mickey of vodka?" I smiled and said, "Sure, sounds good, how will we get it none` of us are eighteen?" Nancy said, "I have someone that said he would pick it up for us." I said "Okay, does Patricia know?" "Yeah, Patricia knows." she said with a giggle." I said, "See you soon, I am so excited this is going to be fun." and hung up the phone.

I loved spending time with my friends, they made me happy, Cody was not going to be there tonight, and we are drinking vodka. I double checked myself in the mirror, quickly went down the stairs, grabbed my shoes and quietly opened the door, closing it just as quietly. I slipped on my shoes and left. I did not care what Cody was doing or had planned. I did not like him, and I did not want to hang out with him.

Walking across the street I took a deep breath in, looked up, smiling saying, "Freedom." Feeling like a weight was lifted off my shoulders, giggling. I ran to Patricia's bus stop, thinking, I have not felt this good since summertime, Cody needed to go. Once at Patricia's bus stop, I sat down, kicking my feet out and squealing as I laughed, "Cody doesn't know I left or where I am."

Patricia walked up to the bus stop and said in a surprised voice, "Autumn what are you doing here?" I said, "I was ready early and just decided to walk over here to meet you instead." Patricia looked at me with a smile saying, "I am so excited this is going to be so much fun." I said "Yay." I asked Patricia "What are we mixing the vodka with?" Patricia said, "I don't know, maybe we should run to the store really quickly to get some pop."

We got back to the bus stop and Patricia lit a cigarette just in time for the bus to arrive. She flicked the cherry off, we hopped onto the bus and walked to the back to sit with Nancy, we laughed and giggled. Nancy opened her bag, there before us was a clear bottle with black writing that said, Silent Sam. Patricia and I both looked at each other, our eyes were big but our smiles were bigger, "We are going to have so much fun." Said Patricia. Returning the excitement when I said, "I know."

Bailey, and Paige where waiting for us when we got off the bus. We smiled, then screamed. "Ahhh, this is going to be awesome," Walking around the corner to go to the community hall Paige and Bailey squealed, "We have Peach schnapps." Nancy blurted, "No way, we have Silent Sam." Instead of mixing it with pop we took turns drinking the Silent Sam out of the bottle. I did not eat that day, so the booze kicked in much quicker. Wow! It was a great feeling. I had a smile from ear to ear. No problems, no cares in the world.

We walked into the hall, Nancy looked at me and Patricia and started to scream, Whaoooh! Excitement written on her face. I asked, "Who is this?" Nancy responded, "Heavy D & the boyz, Somebody for me." Nancy bounced her way onto the dance floor and started dancing, we quickly followed. The alcohol was kicking in quickly and the music was so good. I was feeling great, so was everybody else.

The music had a great beat and most of it was unfamiliar. It was my first introduction to rap, hip hop, and R&B at a dance, I enjoyed it. Just then Technetronic Pump up the jam came on while we were all dancing on the floor and three girls came on the dance floor to join us, two white girls, and one Milano. Nancy, Patricia, Bailey, and Paige all seemed to know who the girls were. They all started to cheer as we continued to dance.

The song ended, we all left the dance floor and walked straight outside, Nancy quickly introduced me. "Autumn this is Rhonda, Leah, and Becky, this is Autumn. "We all smiled and said "Hi." We quickly opened our mickeys out and passed them around. Nancy opened her pack of cigarettes and offered me one. The music played in the background. We all stood outside finishing what was left of our micky, dancing, laughing, having an awesome time.

Don't, don't, don't, don't believe the hype" played through on the speakers, everybody started to scream, quickly putting their cigarettes out, running inside to go dance. When we danced, we all danced the same, it looked like we were climbing the wall. A Milano girl danced her way into the circle, her head bobbing side to side. She was a bigger girl wearing baggy pants, turtleneck, and black sweater with Adidas written across her chest and her hair styled high. We all continued to dance. I felt numb from the alcohol. I danced my way over to the center of the circle saying, "I feel great, this is so much fun."

The dance had ended, everybody started to empty out of the hall and waited at the bus stop. I asked Nancy "Can I spend the night at your house?" Nancy said "Sure." Nancy looked at Patricia and said, "You can too." Patricia said "OK." It was eleven o'clock when we arrived at Nancy's place and the effects of the booze wore off. We laid in bed talking about all the people we saw, and how we are going to all the dances from now on.

My mission, seeing less of Cody, with school, work, and friends at should be possible. At night I would sleep with my mom. Sometimes Cody would not come home, most nights though he did and pulled me out of bed into my bedroom to have his way with me, I stopped protesting because it got me nowhere. Lying there waiting for Cody to be done.

Afterwards I would go for a shower, turning the water on as hot as my body could handle it, for as long as I could. I tried to wash away the filth. I could not understand why mom would not do anything. I hated being at home, the thought of leaving mom made me sad, I was all she had. Sometimes when Mom got her welfare cheque Cody would go with her to the mall, and I hated it because I thought that he was taking advantage of her, and her disability. Cody used to work at a toy store but has not been working for a while. I tried to talk to her, but she did not listen to what I had to say.

CHAPTER 8
Happy Birthday Baby!

Valentine's day arrived, Cody came into my bedroom while I was sitting on the floor in front of the mirror, getting ready for bed. He was holding twelve red roses, "Happy Valentine's Day." Cody said as he handed me the roses, grabbing my head, pulling me in for a passionate kiss, sticking his tongue down my throat like the first time he kissed me in the mall. All I could do is think gross.

Cody put the roses on the dresser and asked, "Where is my gift?" I looked at Cody as if he already knew the answer. I did not get him anything, he was not my valentine. I wanted him to go away. Cody said, "Did you even get me a birthday gift?" His birthday was within a few days of Valentine's Day, I just looked away. Cody looked at my pajama pants, having a hole in them from when Cody pushed me to the floor, he grabbed them and said, "I hate these pants." He tore them all the way down to the seam of the cuff on my right leg. I tried to push Cody away from me. Cody grabbed me and threw me onto the bed and pulled whatever was left of my pajamas off, Cody then ripped my underwear off. I tried to get him off me, but his arms had me pinned down. I started to try and kick him off, he put his weight on me and used his one hand to get his pants down and wiggled around to force my legs apart. Cody then used both of his hands to pin me down. Cody started to thrust really hard and fast, it hurt so bad that my eyes watered. When Cody was done, he rolled over, pulling up his pants leaving his penis and pubic hair revealed.

I could hear mom coming up the stairs, the door opened, mom was standing in the doorway asking, "What are you doing?" I went to get up and Cody reached over and grabbed my pubic hair and said, "Nothing just laying here." I laid back down. Mom said "Oh." and closed the door. Cody turned onto his side and took a good look at my vagina, sounding shocked, saying "Your pubic hair is red." I thought to myself, if you knew anything about me, you would know that I am not naturally a blonde, but red head.

I went to get up, Cody asked, "Where do you think you are going?" "Duh, to bed." I retorted. Cody said, "You are staying here tonight, turn the light off and get back here." Tapped the bed beside him. "I am going for a shower." I said, closing the door behind me. When I was done my shower, Cody was waiting for me outside the door, he grabbed my arm and walked me to my bedroom. I was lying beside Cody, He turned over onto his side to face me, saying, "I can't believe that you didn't get the man that loves you a birthday gift?" I could not say anything I just looked at him. Cody turned back over onto his back and did not say anything else. I was so tired I fell asleep.

When I woke up the next day Cody watched me get ready. It was very creepy. The things he did kept me on my feet all the time, I never knew what he would next, this day he sang, Don't Be Cruel, by Bobby Brown, his eyes following me. When I went into the bathroom, downstairs, he followed me. On the bus Cody sat in the corner looking out the window singing the same song. Looking at Nancy and Patricia with a smile and shrugged my shoulders.

Bailey, and Paige were at the bus terminal when we arrived. Don't Be Cruel kept rolling off Cody's tongue, adding a little dance step side to side, with his hips giving a pop. Bailey looked a Cody with a smile saying, "You are happy today." Cody smiled and said "Yeah." We could not help but all look at each other and smile and giggle. Cody moved behind me and started to brush up against me. A little embarrassed I tried to walk away. He grabbed me and put his arms up over my shoulders, then he started to grind me from behind, he grabbed my hair and tilted my head just enough to be able to whisper in my ear.

Cody was singing and dancing away from my friends making me move with him, quietly singing "Oh girl I loved you but you turned and you walked away, I will love you more tomorrow than I know I do today, you told me that you'd never hurt me, girl you just tore my life apart, tell me baby, why did you do that won't you bring me back my heart." I broke the grip that Cody had on me, I turned and looked at him with confusion. Cody brought his feet together and moved his hips and continued to sing. "You told me that you'd never leave me, girl you just went and told a lie, tell me baby why'd you do it? Why'd you make me want to cry? I felt fear come over me, I could not let him see me cry.

Gathering my composure as I fled towards my friends, Cody followed, dancing his way back to the group, singing the rest of the song, why do you treat me so bad? I smiled and pretended that I wasn't afraid, asking Nancy "What are we doing today?"

Before Nancy could answer Cody stepped in between me and her, opening his mouth, slithering his tongue down my throat where he lingered, saying "My ride's here I'll see you later baby, remember that you are mine!" Cody winked then he clicked his tongue and left.

We all watched Cody walk towards a white sedan with tinted windows. Cody turned around saying, "Autumn you better get to class." We could not see who was in the car, but once inside the car sat there for a few minutes, then backed out and sped off. We stood there looking, and Patricia asked, "Who did Cody just leave with?" I said, "I don't know." Bailey said, "That is Curtis." "He hangs out with Justin" She paused saying "That is bad news." Paige quickly said, "Yeah, bad news."

I shivered, my stomach turning into knots, putting my hand across my stomachs whispering, "Nothing is right about Cody." Saying louder, "I know it." the girls looked at me and Patricia said, "Know what?" I looked at her with sadness in my eyes and said "Nothing." I did not know what to expect, I just knew that there was something very wrong with Cody and hair on the back of my neck stood up.

We did not get on the bus to go to school, walking towards the bus shelter to discuss what we are going to do today. The warmth of the heaters warmed me up and eased the knots in my stomach. We sat down on the seats and I looked at the girls and thought I am the oldest of all of them. I wanted to discuss what Cody was doing to me, but I was too scared, maybe they would not believe me. Then I started thinking about my oldest brother Dave, and how he was only a few years older than me and the things that he has sheltered me from. I thought about the time we walked across the fields in our old town, by the high school. We went to the Pharmacy and food stored; Dave took a toy toaster with pretend toast for me. I was hungry and we got halfway across the field he opened his jacket and said "Here, when you get hungry you can make yourself some toast." My eyes lit up, saying, "Thank you." Giving him a big hug. It was freezing so we quickly walked across the field towards home.

I heard "Autumn are you listening?" I said "Sorry, what did you say?" Bailey knocked in the air saying "Hello, anybody there, McFly?" We all started to laugh and could not stop laughing. Nancy said, "Bailey knows where we could go hang out, are you up for it?" I said "Yeah." We pooled all our money together and we had a total of thirty-five dollars between the five of us to get some alcohol.

As we waited for the bus this tall skinny guy, with dark wavy hair, pimples all over his face, walked into the bus terminal. He looked kind of out of it and then he noticed Bailey and Paige. He said "Hey!" we all sat there while Bailey said "Hi." and continued the conversation, Bailey finally said "Kaleb, do you have any hash, don't fucking lie to me you mother fucker." Paige piped up, "Yeah, we know that you have some." Patricia, Nancy, and I sat there shocked, mouths slightly open. Kaleb said, "Yeah I have some, how much do you want?" Bailey said, "We have twenty-five dollars." Kaleb said, "It is fifteen dollars for one gram or two for twenty-five." Bailey said "OK, give us two grams."

Bailey turned and looked at us and said, "Come here." We followed her to the other side of the terminal and Bailey held out her hand and said, "Give me the money." We all reached into our pockets and school bags and pulled out the money. Bailey took the money and said, "thanks, we are getting high." walked to Kaleb and handed him twenty-five dollars. Kaleb reached into his pocket and pulled out two baggies and handed them to Bailey. Bailey took the baggies and said, "It better be all there." Kaleb said, "It is, don't worry." Bailey lifted the baggies and there were a small little greyish, greenish rectangle about an inch in each bag. Nancy, Patricia, and I looked at each other, shocked and our mouths slightly open.

Bailey walked over to us and said, "Let's go girls." A bus pulled up and we all got on it and went to the back of the bus to sit down. Nancy pointed and said "Look." We all looked and in big black permanent marker was written "Kiss N Cas." it took up half of the seat. Everybody looked at me and I said, "I didn't write that." The bus pulled out forcing us to sit down. We approached some town houses; Bailey pulled the bell and the bus stopped we got off and followed Bailey up to one of the doors.

Bailey knocked on the door and a tall girl with brown wavy hair and blue eyes came to the door. Bailey said, "Hi Tracy, can we come in?" Tracy said "Sure." There was a tall, handsome young man with dark hair about eighteen standing there. He was about six feet tall. Bailey looked at the two and introduced us, and then said, "This is Tom and Tracy." We smiled saying, "Hi." Bailey walked to the kitchen, turned the stove on and put two knives on the burner, she opened the cupboard and took a plate out and sat at the table. Bailey pulled the baggy out of her pocket and took one of the rectangles out and started to cut them into little pieces. Paige put them on the plate. We all knew that it was hash but none of us have done it before. We laughed and giggled wondering what it was like. Patricia's eyes got big saying, "My mom is going to be so mad at me because I am skipping school, I can't go home stoned." We all giggled.

Bailey took the plate and walked over to the stove, she had an empty two-liter pop bottle with the bottom cut off from under the sink and asked, "Who wants to go first?" No body moved, Paige saying, "I'll go first." Paige gripped the cut-up pop bottle, placing the spout to her lips. Bailey grabbed a knife in each hand and tapped the red, hot knife on one of the balls of hash placed on the plate, slowly moved it under the pop bottle and touched the knives together and smiled and said" Blades." Paige sucked back all the smoke until it was gone, held it in and then blew the smoke out.

Bailey scrapped the knives together then placed them back on the burner saying, "I will go next." Paige did the knives while Bailey took her turn. We looked at each other, talking about how we were nervous, who was going next. Nancy could not stop laughing. I turned and looked at Nancy asking, "why are you laughing you haven't even tried it yet?" Nancy said, "I can't help it." Patricia said, "Nancy always laughs when she is scared." That is weird I thought, I am scared and had anxiety, but I did not laugh. Nancy gave me a little push and said, "You go next." I quickly said "No." Bailey looked at Tom and Tracy asking, "Do you want to go next?" They nodded. Tom went first, then Tracy. I looked at Bailey saying, "I will go next." I walked over put my lips over the bottle and took a deep breath in, held it for a couple of seconds, then blew it out. Nancy had her turn, she inhaled, and started coughing, Patricia giggled as stood there waiting her turn, Nancy and I stood there anticipating something to happen.

Tom went and got his ghetto blaster and started to play Guns 'N' Roses, Welcome to The Jungle. I could not help but giggle.

Each taking turns as we went through the line up again. The music got louder, and louder as we sat there laughing and talking about stupid things. We were having so much fun. Finally, the moment we have been waiting for has arrived. "I am really stoned, I cannot go home like this, my mom is going to know." Patricia blurted. The giggling stopped for a moment, we all turned our gaze to her, Bailey suddenly said "Fuuuck!" It was like we were in a room full of laughing gas, we all started to laugh hysterically.

Tom just watched all us girls quietly, then he got up and said, "Bailey come and do the blades for me." Patricia asked, "Seriously, what time is it, I can't go home stoned, my mom is going to know." We were so stoned we started to laugh again. Tom looked at the clock on the stove saying, "It is ten o'clock." We were holding our stomachs laughing, on the verge of tearing up. I stopped laughing for a moment, with a serious face I looked at Patricia saying, "let's do another blade."

Through our laughter we managed to make our way by the stove, each of us inhaling another blade. Tom was sitting at the table rolling a joint, after our turn we all sat down. Tom lit the joint and passed it around. When it got to Patricia, she said "I have never done this before." Nancy looked at Patricia and said in a high-pitched voice, with her eyebrows raised "I know, Me neither." The joint went around, and around, stopping on Patricia, she looked serious when she stated, "Again, I just had it, did you guys even have a turn?"

Tom started to play Parents Just Don't Understand, by DJ Jazzy Jeff and the Fresh Prince, Nancy lip sang, our laughter did not subside. Bailey said "Fuck, why is everything so funny? Paige quickly answering, "I do not know!" Patricia looking sad said,

"I am hungry!" Even that was funny, we laughed at everything. Finally, it got to be lunch time and there was a Seven eleven straight down the road.

The journey to seven eleven took what felt like forever, we kept stopping because we were laughing so much. We bought hamburgers, chips, chocolate bars, and Slurpee's, sat outside the store enjoying the food. Patricia held her hamburger in front of her eyes, studying it intensely, saying, "I did not know that seven eleven hamburgers are so good." Bailey changed Patricia's attention when she pointed at a white house with black trim saying, "Dude I live right there, my mom is going to see me, we need to go." Once back at Tom's house we let ourselves come down from the high, my stomach started to feel knots again. All of us girls sat in the kitchen cohering, we had so much fun, we decided we were meeting at Tom's of Friday before the dance to get stoned.

Cody was not home when I arrived, mom did not notice that I was high, if she did, she did not say anything. Cody came in just as I was putting spaghetti that I made on a plate for myself. Offering, "Cody are you hungry, I made spaghetti, do you want some?" Cody looked at me with disgust, angrily answering, "No, you know I am a diabetic, I can't eat that." Swooping up my plate, I enjoyed my spaghetti while watching tv.

I must have fallen asleep; I was falling and awoke to Cody pulling me off the couch. He said, "It is time for bed, we are going now." Still groggy I walked up the stairs and went into the bathroom to get ready for bed. Walking into Mom's room looking at the clock, it was just after midnight. I was tired, I fell back asleep. I felt like I was being pulled again, pulling myself away I turned over, Cody grabbed my arm hard, pulling me with some force. I gasped, Cody sternly said, "Shh." Giving me a tug. I staggered as Cody pulled me towards my bedroom. Cody threw me on the bed, pulling my pants off, sliding on top of me. Separating myself from Cody, I closed my eyes praying, "God, I love you, give me comfort, please help me." Turning into requests, "Why is he doing this to me? Please take me out of this."

Cody stopped, rolled over, falling asleep. Lying there a tear rolled down the side of my face, I wiped it away. Turning onto my side, my arm under my head looking at Cody's naked body as he slept. The light was shining through the room from the hallway. Mom was afraid of the dark, she would never admit it though. I could not help but think, Cody's body looked so mature, his chest was like a man's chest, his build was bigger than both of my brothers, who were about the same age. His arms were big and toned like he worked out and his legs were the same. Weird.

I awoke to Cody giving me a kiss with his tongue down my throat. Cody's breath was so bad I almost threw up, Cody moved back as if I slapped him angrily saying, "Why are you such a bitch, do you know how many girls would love to be with me?" "Bitch, do you know how lucky you are?" Cody moved towards the bed towering over me, moving an inch away from my face, quietly whispering "Do you know who I am?" "Well it is about time you find out." Storming out of the room, straight to the bathroom.

My heart felt like a lightning bolt of ice just struck it, I was paralyzed. The thought that went through my mind was, you are evil, you spoiled me for my husband, I am used goods. The tears rolled down my face, I looked up saying "God, there is nothing else that Cody could do to me." Cody stormed into the bedroom, giving me a cold look, flying towards me, slamming his hand down beside my face, the pressure pulling my hair. Cody moved closer to my face, his eyes dark, saying through his teeth, "Why are you crying bitch?" "Stop crying right now." He gently kissed my lips and left.

I wiped the tears from my face, took a deep breath in, saying with determination "God, there is nothing at this point that Cody could do, that is worse than what he has already done." I crawled out of bed and got ready for school. My stomach was in knots, I kept looking to see if Cody was lurking, thankfully he was not. When I awoke the next morning, I kicked the blankets off moving quickly downstairs, wondering if Cody slept downstairs, he did not come home.

CHAPTER 9
Because of you

Friday at school Dan came and found me outside the doors where we smoke, he smiled saying, "Hi Autumn, can you come to my locker, I have something for you." Nancy and Patricia looked at me smiling, "Sure." I said, following him upstairs, Dan opened his locker asking, "Are you OK, I haven't seen you for a while." I smiled saying, "Yeah I am fine. How are you doing?" Dan said, "I am doing really good, I saw this, and I thought of you." He pulled out a book and a cassette tape, handing it to me. It was an autobiography of Paula Abdul, and the forever your girl soundtrack. I looked at Dan surprised saying, "Thank you!" I gave him a quick hug, saying, "That is very thoughtful." "You still want to be a dancer, right?" Dan asked inquisitively, smiling I nodded when I said, "Yeah." "I have to get to class now, don't be a stranger, I miss seeing you." Were the words I heard as Dan walked away.

I watched Dan walk down the hallway, then disappear. Standing there looking at the book, A locker slammed moving my attention in the direction. There was that Milano girl from the Community Hall dance. I smiled saying, "Hi." She looked at me, took a deep sigh in, spreading her fingers apart and shook her hands in the air, frantically saying, "Hi." with a distressed giggle. To get her attention I said, "My name is Autumn, I saw you at the dance." She smiled and looked a little insecure and said "Yeah, I am Tammy." "Sorry, I'm living in foster care and my foster mom is a fucking bitch, I hate it there." I said, "There is a dance tonight are you going?" Tammy paused and said "Yeah, maybe." I said "OK" "Well maybe I will see you then." We left to class.

Nancy, Patricia, and I discussed our plans for tonight. Patricia and I were telling our Moms that we were spending the night at Nancy's. Nancy's parents were going out to an anniversary party with some family friend's, so they were not going to be home until late. We were just going home to eat and get ready, then I would walk to Patricia's and we would meet Nancy on the bus to go to Tom's where Bailey and Paige were meeting us.

The dance and it was rocking. Tammy showed up as well, we danced all night, only taking cigarette breaks. Towards the end of the night Nancy danced around the circle and whispered in our ears "Don't look, but there are two girls standing there that have been staring at us all night." Continuing to dance; we each took a turn to look at the two girls. One had long almost platinum blonde hair with a tight black dress and boots that went up to her thighs. The other had dirty blonde hair below her shoulders, high boots, and a tight skirt that showed off her skinny legs, tiny waist, and thighs so big that they looked like they belonged to a different body. None of us knew who they were, so we just kept dancing.

We were still high as we made our way on the bus to go to Nancy's. we were the only ones on the bus besides a young boy with light brown curly hair our age, making his way to his destination. He sat down on the same seat as me but on the opposite side of the seat. We laughed and giggled, the bus came to a stop at the bus stop, two black guys got on the bus, we didn't even notice until we heard the guy beside me yelling "No, no, no." It scared me, I turned and looked, the back door opened, the two black guys pulled the guy off the bus, the doors slammed shut and the bus sped off. We ran to the back window and watched the two black guys beat up the guy that was sitting beside me. We looked at each other in shock. Patricia said "Weird." Nancy and I agreed. Feeling a little scared we quickly walked to Nancy's without saying a word to each other.

Saturday night, Cody showed up towards the end of my shift. I was shocked, I have not seen Cody in couple of days, he has never been to my work. "What are you doing here?" I asked surprised. Cody said, "I wanted to make sure that you come home tonight." I retorted, "I am hanging out with my friends tonight." Cody replied more like an order than request, "No, we are going home, I will be right here waiting for you." He pointed to a chair beside the wall, sat until I was done work. Once outside Cody grabbed my arm and said, "Just in case you forgot, you belong to me and you are going home."

When Nancy phoned, she wondered, "What happened to you last night?" I said, "Cody showed up at work and wanted me to go home." Nancy changed to subject saying, "Sean and his friend picked me and Patricia up last night, in a stolen vehicle." "They dropped us off and got into a high-speed chase with police and got arrested." "Wow, I am glad I wasn't there." I exclaimed. Cody was listening behind me, I heard "You are not going anywhere, you are staying home," Cody grabbed the phone and hung it up.

Cody stood in front of me, making eye contact, slyly saying, "Who is Brandy?" I shrugged my shoulders saying, "I do not know." Cody tilted his head as he continued, "You must know who she is, you pissed her off, she is after you, when she finds you, she is going to kick your ass." I rolled my eyes and shook my head no saying, "I don't know who Brandy is, I have never met her." Cody smiled mischievously saying, "Well she knows you and is going to kick the shit out of you." "She is very pissed off at you, I do not know what you did, you better watch out." "What did you do?" I anxiously asked, "Who is she?" Cody replied, "She is a hoe." Convinced I responded, "Obviously you are thinking of the wrong person." Cody looked confirming, "You better watch it, she is mad and is going to kick your ass and I can't stop her." I sighed, taking a deep breath in, feeling my stomach started to knot up. I said, "She must have me mistaken for somebody else." Cody shrugged his shoulders not changing his mind saying, "She seems to think it is you!"

Cody left immediately; I took the opportunity to call Nancy back. Nancy was giving me the play by play of the events that occurred the night before and how they were all high, Nancy and Patricia both got grounded. After she was done talking, I slipped the question, "Who is Brandy?" Nancy said, "I found out that she is one of the hoe's staring at us at the dance, remember?" Responding, "Yeah, I don't know her." Nancy ranted, "Brandy was at the dance with another hoe Sam." "Sam likes Sean, she better stay not go near him, or I am going to kick her ass." Inquiring, "Did I do something that I am not aware of, Cody said that Brandy is after me and is going to kick the shit out of me." Nancy chuckled, "No, nothing all we did was dance and have fun, we don't even know who she is." "Why don't I feel better?" I wondered out loud. I heard a whisper, "I have to go before I get in trouble." Hanging up the phone.

It has been a few days and Cody has not been around, when we were at bus terminal Cody showed up with a couple of guys, I have seen before in passing but had never talked to them. Cody franticly ran to me freaking out and saying, "What are you doing here, you better get out of here. Brandy is coming and she is going to kick your ass." I waited with Nancy and Patricia for our bus, I was feeling anxiety. I was really scared, Nancy asked, "What did you do?" Stressed out answering her, "I don't know, nothing that I know of, I have never met her, I didn't know who she was until you told me." Finally, our bus came, and we went home.

I thought of ways I could avoid Brandy, places, or change the time I was leaving. I feared Brandy, a girl I do not even know. Stomping my foot as I mumbled, "Why do I have to change my life?" Now walking a little further to take a different bus to school, hoping she would forget about kicking my ass. Cody still came to the house occasionally and pulled me out of bed in the middle of the night. One morning after Cody kept me up half of the night, I woke up late, Cody was already gone. I quickly got ready and ran out to the bus stop.

Worried that I missed my bus, I turned and looked at a young guy I never seen before, noticing that he had a watch on. He was tall and skinny, with dark hair. Casually I asked, "Excuse me, do you know what time it is?" He looked at his watch and said, "It is." We both turned to look because we heard tires screeching. A white sedan with tinted windows sped around the corner and came to a sudden stop in front of us. Two black guys got out of the vehicle and grabbed the guy standing beside me and started punching, kicking, and kneeing him. They were yelling "You mother fucker, who do you think you are? Don't look at her, don't talk to her, and don't you ever go near her again, we will fuck you up, you mother fucker." They let go of him and he fell to the ground. Unable to move, still in shock.

Cody grabbed me, pulled me to the car, the other guy opened the door, Cody threw me in the back seat. Cody was over me, his face an inch away from mine. My back was against the driver's side, back passenger door. Cody was yelling "You fucking bitch, who in the fuck was that? You are mine! Who the fuck, do you think you are? You fucking bitch! I could not make out what he was saying after a while I was so scared; my head was spinning. The car came to a stop and Cody got out of the car, he grabbed me and pulled me out with him, throwing me to the ground, closing the door, hopping in the front passenger side of the car and drove off.

My heart was beating fast, a little embarrassed I looked around to see if anyone saw anything. My adrenalin was raging, feeling scared, I had to think, where am I? Realizing that they threw me out on the side doors of the school. Whispering, "What just happened, don't cry, don't cry." I stood up, grabbed my composure, and walked around to the front of the school where Nancy and Patricia were standing outside having a cigarette. Smiling I said, "Hi, can I have a drag?" Nancy handed me a cigarette asking, "Where were you?" recalling the events in my head, I answered, "Cody's friend gave me a ride." Nancy said "Must be nice. I said sarcastically "Real nice."

I could not concentrate in class; my stomach was in knots. I placed my fingertips on my forehead because I had a headache, and I was shaking so bad. On the break I met Nancy, and Patricia outside at the doors, lying when I mentioned, "I have a doctor's appointment, so I am leaving." I was going to go and just see if I could get in without an appointment. Nancy said, "We will catch the bus with you and meet up at Tom's later."

We transferred buses at bus terminal, the bus was pulling out, Nancy pointed saying, "Hey there is Brandy, and Sam." Nancy placed her hand against the window and gave them the middle finger. Thankfully, they were busy talking and not facing us. Nancy did her head bob saying, "Fucking hoes." In a high-pitched voice I asked, "Why would you do that, Brandy wants to kick my ass, I don't even know her," Nancy giggled replying, "Because they are fucking hoes."

Nancy and Patricia got off the bus before me and I continued to Lake mall where my doctor's office was. Thankfully when I got there, I was able to see him. I sat in the room waiting, trying to build up the courage to talk to him about Cody. There was a light knock on the door. Dr. Gere walked in and said with a concerned voice. "Hi, Autumn, what brings you in today?" He had blonde hair, blue eyes with a slim build and he looked like he just graduated from medical school. I blurted "My stomach hurts and I have a sore throat and can barely talk." He responded, "Let's take a look." He took the light and looked in my ears and throat. "Humm, lay down and I will look at your abdominal region." He felt around and did not feel anything. He helped me up saying, "I do not see anything, how long has this been going on for?" In a defeated voice I said, "A while." He said, "If you don't feel better come back and see me." I nodded asking, "Could I please get a note for school?" Dr. Gere pulled out his notepad and wrote the note and tore it off saying, "Take care Autumn." Leaving the room. I wanted to tell him about Cody, but I was overcome by fear and shame, like he would believe me.

Walking through the parking lot to get to the Lake Bus Terminal I looked up asking, "God, how could I be so stupid? I just had a chance to tell my doctor and I did not, please help me. This is bigger than me, God you need to help me." The feeling I had in my stomach said it all, I cannot cry because it is a sign of weakness, tears will not get me through this. I could not help but look around me, wondering what is going to happen next? I could not see Curtis's white car, Brandy or Cody anywhere, so I quickly walked over and tried to blend in with people waiting for their bus.

My cares disappeared when I got to Tom's I really loved my friends, everything seemed easy with them. Looking towards the kitchen it was smoky, Every little step by Bobby Brown was playing, you could hear talking, and laughing. Taking off my shoes, saying "Hello." I recognized Bailey's voice when she said, "Autumn what are you waiting for, blades." I smiled and thought wow, this is great Cody does not know where I am, and I am safe with my friends.

This past week had been incredibly stressful, everywhere I went I just missed Brandy, she was hot on my trail. When I was at the bus Terminal Kyle Brooks came up to me saying, "Cody was just here with Brandy, they are looking for you." Kyle has been hanging out with Cody lately, he is Milano. His hair is dark blonde and curly, he has a box cut like Will Smith, freckles all over his body. Cody calls him a "Gangsta wanna be." He is only about thirteen.

Dakota and Luc were at the mall when we went for lunch, their eyes were red, and they looked stoned. Luc never said anything to me, and his eyes scared me, they were dark, they would follow me. Sometimes I found myself thinking, Luc does not hate me. Occasionally I saw Luc with Cody, but I was never introduced to him, Cody always did the talking when he was with Luc. Where Luc was, Curtis was close by. The closest I got to Curtis was that day they beat up the boy because I asked him for the time. Everything happened so fast I did not get a good look at him; I cannot say for sure that is even Curtis.

I looked around to see if Curtis or Cody were creeping in the background. My heart was beating fast, all I wanted to do was cry. Instead, I stood there shaking my leg to hide my whole body shaking. Dakota gave a little chuckle asking, "Is there anything wrong?" I quickly said, "No, I have an assignment due. I am going back to school to finish it. I will see you later." Dakota laughed saying, "You know you will." Looking to Luc, they chuckled. I turned around to leave and Luc said, "We will see you later." I have never heard Luc say anything before, it gave me the chills. I stood up straight like the hair on the back of my neck, continuing to walk out the doors.

My eyes wondered to see if there was a white car around anywhere. I did not see one that looked like the one that Curtis drove. Collapsing against the wall holding my stomach, it was starting to get sore, I took a deep breath in saying, "God help me, I am scared, I have to keep looking over my shoulder all the time." I bolted to the bus stop, hopped on the bus to take me to the bus terminal. As I walked to the back of the bus, I could not help but notice a white car turn in behind the bus. I quickly sat down in the first seat that I could, sliding down so I could not see out the window. All I wanted to do was disappear. I looked up saying, "God take me out of this."

After the bus made a few detours I slowly moved my way up, discreetly looking out the back window to see if Curtis's car was still behind the bus. I did not see the car, so I sat up and thought about the closest bus stop to my house before it approached bus terminal. It is about fifteen blocks away from home, pulling the bell and got off the bus and walked home through the army base. As I walked, I pleaded with God, "I need you right now, I am so scared. I am so tired, I feel alone, Please, please help me."

Nobody was home when I arrived, I took the opportunity to have a nap before work, I had not been getting much sleep lately, exhaustion is what I felt, my pillow welcomed me. Feeling refreshed on my walk to work, it was chilly walking home, I was glad that I dressed warm, and with walking fast it felt like spring was almost here. Crossing the street to go home and I could hear music, as I got closer, I could make out the words, it was Eazy E, Boyz N the Hood. I thought, no, running up to the house I opened the door, the house was foggy and smelled of pot, you could get high off the fumes. There are people everywhere, mostly black. I recognized almost everybody. How is there a party at my house and I do not know about it.

Frantically I made my way through the crowd until I found my mom. She was wasted, angrily I asked, "Mom, how could you let this happen?" She looked at me and took a drag of the joint just passed to her by Luc and blew the smoke in my face, then passed me the joint. Clenching my teeth, with fury I said "No." Mom totally wasted slurred, "Fuck." Looking around the table laughing. I looked around and Cody was nowhere to be found, Bailey,

Patricia, Paige, and Tammy, were drinking and getting high in the living room. Bailey saw me happily saying, "Fuck Autumn your mom rocks." I was so frustrated, not knowing what to do I stormed outside, walking to the park across the street.

Patricia, Bailey, and Paige followed me. I grabbed the pole on the equipment and started to twirl as I held back my tears. Looking at Patricia I wondered, "Who planned the party?" Patricia said, "Cody and your mom, you did not know?" Bailey reached into her pocket and pulled out a joint, lit it and passed it to me saying, "Here." Taking the joint, inhaling, then exhaling saying "I had no idea." Patricia said "I thought you were getting ready for it when you left school. Dakota and Luc told us at lunch that there was a party at your house." The gangster rap was getting louder, so I said, "We better go inside."

NWA Fuck the Police was loud and clear, Dakota and Luc were in the kitchen, Dakota was dancing, jumping up throwing his arms in the air shouting, "FUK DA POLICE!" Annoyed I walked over to the ghetto blaster, turning it down. Mom yelled in a high-pitched voice "Autumn fucking leave the music alone alright." She stormed over and turned the music back up saying, "Fuck Autumn smarten up eh." as she nodded her head yeah determinately. I was shocked, I turned the music back down and her right hand made a fist and she moved towards me to hit me, I moved, and she missed and stumbled. It got quiet for a second then everybody roared in laughter. Dakota had his jacket hanging off his right shoulder and his right hand held onto the zipper just over his chest. He swung his right shoulder and hip doing a gangster walk towards the ghetto blaster stopped, looked at me, then kissed his teeth cussing, "Bitch." He turned the music back up and started to dance. I went and sat with Patricia, Bailey, and Paige and Tammy asking, "Where is Nancy?" "She is still grounded." Baily stated.

It was getting late, Eazy E Cruisin in my sixty-four was playing, the crowd was starting to clear thankfully, but I still have not seen Cody. My eyes were getting heavy, so I went and turned the music down, mom was passed out on the couch, I stood there and looking at her. I did not recognize her, I felt embarrassment and pity, anger for what she was putting me through. Shutting my feelings off I went upstairs and fell asleep.

I could hear voices in the room, my eyes slowly opened, there were two police officers standing in front of the closet talking to Cody, who was sitting on the sideboard of the waterbed. Dakota, and Luc were sitting on the other side. Still groggy one of the police officers said "Autumn, we got a call from Nancy's parents, Nancy ran away, they think that she is here." "I worked last night and came home to a party, but Nancy wasn't here, I haven't seen her." I replied. The police officer said, "If you see her tell her to go home, her parents are worried about her." I answered concerned, "Of course." The police officers left, I turned and looked at Cody. "Don't worry Nancy is OK." Cody said. The closet doors opened, Nancy came out, jumping out of bed I gave Nancy a hug asking, "Is everything OK?" Nancy said "Yeah, I just had a fight with my parents." Suddenly, Dakota laugh saying, "What the fuck." I turned and looked, Dakota reached on the nightstand and grabbed a big bag of pot laughing when he said, "The fucking Po Po did not see that?" Luc started laughing grabbing the bag out of his hand. My eyes got big, I stormed to the bathroom, slammed the door, locking it behind me.

Cody, Dakota, Luc, and Nancy were gone when I got out of the shower. Mom was sitting at the kitchen table having a coffee and cigarette. I was so angry at her I was starting to hate her; she is supposed to be an adult. I could not help but give her the evil eye, the evidence of last night was everywhere. Mom did not even look at me, just said, "Autumn clean up this mess." "Fuck you, your party you clean it." I snapped, "I hate you for what you have done to me and are allowing." Running upstairs I grabbed my bag and jacket, mom was standing at the front door looking at me as if to say, I dare you. I walked past her, she tried to grab me, but I moved out of her reach, running out the back door, she was not fast enough.

I walked into the Convenience Store, bought a Pepsi, sat at the bus stop waiting. When the bus came, I got on and transferred at different bus terminals, I just rode the bus all day. Having cooled down, I then stopped in at the Bakery to order a birthday cake for mom's birthday next Saturday.

My boss knew immediately I was upset, she looked at me with concern asking "Autumn, your mom has been calling, is everything OK?" Her blue eye's softened, she has always been sweet to me, makes a point to come and talk to me every shift. Unable to make eye contact I said "Yeah, it will be, if she calls again tell her I didn't show up for work please." She walked over and gave me a hug, saying, "What is wrong? Do you need a place to stay tonight?" I smiled at her saying, "Maybe." My shift ended, I stood by the office, Amy opened the door. I asked, "Would you mind if I stayed with you tonight?" Smiling through her words, "I just need to close up, go to the back and wait until I am done."

I waited outside the door as Amy set the alarm, we walked to her car, there were no words exchanged. Amy pulled out of the parking lot and Curtis's car drove around to the back of the building. Careful not to anything out loud, my voice inside was saying, "Thank you Jesus." We got to Amy's and her husband was sitting on the couch. I have met him before at work when he came in to see Amy. Amy said, "Autumn is staying here tonight." He just nodded his head and went back to watching TV. Amy lead me down the hallway and opened a door saying, "You can stay in here, the bathroom is across the hall and if you need anything let me know." "Thank you." I replied, Amy closed the door and left.

The room was obviously a girl's room. Amy had children but they were all grown. I looked at the lace bed skirt on the double sized bed and the cozy floral comforter. I took a deep sigh and hopped into bed. As I laid there I started to pray, I was so tired and relaxed that I did not even finish praying. I woke to a knock on the door, Amy peeked inside saying, "Good morning, I put a towel in the bathroom for you." "Thank you."

When I came out of the bathroom Amy had pancakes on the table, "Come and eat." She sang. I sat down, it was just Amy and me. "I will give you a ride home after we eat." She said, I smiled and said, "Thank you." Thinking this would be a good time to ask, I blurted the question, "Do you think I could pick up extra shifts?" I could read Amy's face, she was concerned when she asked again, "Is everything OK?" I nodded my head yes as I put butter and syrup on my pancakes. I quietly sat there eating, only saying, "Thank you." When I got out of the car.

The house was partially cleaned when I got home, I went upstairs and had a shower and stayed in my room for the rest of the day reading. It was peaceful, nobody here except me and mom. Mom came upstairs and opened my door pretending to be shocked I was home, hoping to get some type of ideal of my feelings when she said, "Oh, you are home?" I did not respond, she closed the door and left.

I must have fallen asleep and awoke to the phone ringing, mom opened my door handing me the phone uttering, "Autumn the phone." It was Amy, confirming my shifts for the week, giving me the weekend off. "Thank you." I said and hung up the phone. "Who is that?" Mom questioned, I was still angry with her, I ignored her, mom did get my attention when she asked, "How much money do you have?" "I don't have money for rent." Knowing where her money went, I replied, "You just got your cheque." "It is gone, I spent it all." She said, I could not even look at her when I shut her down by saying, "No, I have money for the bills I pay." She pleaded, "Can you buy me some cigarettes?" Pretending that she did not just ask me that, I walked by her, got some things, and left.

Mom was known for being the cool mom, skipping school and going to work became my routine. Cody regularly had his way with me, mom in the room down the hall. It was late and I just got home from work, all I wanted to do was sleep, I was tired physically and emotionally. Cody grabbed me and led me to my room, I never knew what to expect from him next. He closed the door, grabbed my hair saying, "Don't fuck with me, I want know where you have been." Cody leaned in and gently kissed my lips; Cody took his shirt off, unbuttoned his pants and they dropped to the floor. Pushing me to the bed, taking my pants off, sliding on top of me. Closing my eyes, I prayed, "God I am sixteen, could this be your will for me." All I felt was dirty and shameful, there was no way this was God's will for me. I opened my eyes watching Cody's face while he finished.

It was mom's birthday, I got up early, caught the bus to the mall to pick up her cake. Paige was at the bus terminal when I got there, coming with me to pick up mom's cake. Stepping off the escalator going up I heard, "Finally, there you are you fucking bitch." I turned around and Brandy was standing there with her hands on her hips. I started to shake; I was terrified. Brandy said, "I am going to kick your fucking ass bitch." "I could do it here or outside, your choice, in here everybody will see me kick your nasty ass hoe." I was so embarrassed and scared, I looked around to see the people around me. It was busy and nobody stopped to see what the commotion was. I thought to myself, if she kicks my ass it will be done and over with and I could go on with my life.

I stammered, "Ok, Outside." Brandy stepped toward me pushing me, demanding, "Outside right here right now." Giving me another push. Once outside she kept pushing me until we got to the stairs, I almost fell down the stairs. I stepped down on the landing and Brandy grabbed my hair from behind and started to punch me in the head, she then started to punch me the face. I felt her knee in my ribs and stomach, then she started to punch me in the face again. All along she was swearing at me. She finally stopped, hit me one last time in the face, whispered in my ear, "Bitch."

My head down, I watched as she slithered up the stairs. Falling against the concrete wall, touching my head crying, "Ouch" the uncontrollable tears followed. I heard laughing, looking up, Paige and a girl I never saw before with long brown hair, were standing there. I made eye contact with the stranger, they both turned and walked away. I was so scared I did not even notice anybody else coming outside, now I am just beat up and embarrassed.

I wiped my tears and walked up the stairs, into the mall straight to the bathroom. I had blood on my lip because my tooth cut it. My left eye and cheek bone were red and had a cut in my eyebrow with a little blood on my eyelid. My tears flowed freely as I cleaned the blood off my face. It hurt to breathe. Paige did not say a word when she came into the washroom. She just watched me clean up. I wanted to ask her if she thought that was funny. Instead I walked to the bakery and picked up Mom's cake. I asked the lady in the bakery "Could you please call me a cab?" She said "Sure." I looked at Paige and said, "I will see you later." I could tell she did not know what to do or say, neither did I.

I stood outside to wait for my cab and thought, I am not sure what hurts more, my beat-up body or the humiliation of Cody and what he is putting me through. I only went home to drop off the birthday cake, it still hurt to breath, so I went to the doctor's office. When the doctor came in, he looked at me asking, "What happened to you?" I told him what happened and that it hurt to breathe. As he checked my ribs, he said "You are going to have a nice shiner." "You have a couple of bruised ribs, your nose isn't broken, and no broken teeth. I will give you something for the pain, you rest for a couple of days and you will feel better." My head down I nodded yes.

Right after I dropped my prescription off at the pharmacy, I went to the police station to file charges against Brandy. I thought that if I charged her then she will confirm that Cody was the one who put her up to it. If I press charges, then they will leave me alone. When filling out the statement a question popped in my head, is Cody Brandy's pimp, could not be. On the report I did not know what to call Cody, he is living in my home, having sex with me, he is a boy. He must be my boyfriend. My stomach was feeling very sore and this was occurring more often. I finished the report and went to pick my prescription, going straight home to enjoy birthday cake with mom.

Mom's cake was vanilla with strawberries, I enjoyed it so much I forgot about my wounds for a short period of time, it was comforting my spirit. The phone rang, it was Nancy phoning to see how I was. Paige phoned her and told her what happened. I knew the news was going to travel, I was so embarrassed. I told Nancy what the doctor said and that I charged Brandy, ending the conversation, "I am going to go to bed, could you please tell Patricia.?" Nancy said "Sure." I hung up the phone and walked to the cupboard and opened the container with the pain medication. I took two out and held them in my hand and staring at them, thinking, what if I took the whole bottle? I could end this right now, I would not have feel anything anymore, the pain was starting to get to be too much, I would not have to worry about Cody raping, me or getting beat up anymore by random hoes. I would be safe with Jesus, shaking my head mumbling, "No." "What." Mom asked, my glanced turned to her saying, "I don't want to talk to anybody, I am going to lay down."

It took a while to fall asleep, the phone kept ringing. I could hear mom say, "She is sleeping." then a pause, "OK I will." The tears would not stop falling, the thoughts, it is not too late, you can take the rest of the bottle and end it now. Eventually, exhaustion kicked in, the crying stopped, feeling like I fought a battle I dozed off to sleep. When I turned over I jolted awake from the sharp pain in my ribs, looking at the clock, It was nine PM. Crawling back into bed, humbling myself on my knees, my head dropping after taking the pain killers, being hopeful when I said, "Things will be better tomorrow." Pulling the covers as I fell to the pillow.

It was ten AM, Cody did not come home last night, he was unpredictable. Suddenly, I giggled feeling excited asking God, "Could it be it is over?" My heart sang praises to God, I thanked him. Then I started crying, "God please let this be done, I don't know how much more I can take." My emotions were all over the place, "How much can one person take?"

Winning the emotional battle, being rested, the only thing left to do was to feast, I was starving. After eating I took my medication, mom with her feet on the kitchen table, took a drag of her cigarette, blowing the smoke out demanding, "Autumn go get me some smokes." Counting out the exact amount of money from my bag, throwing it at her feet saying, "No, you smoke, you want cigarettes, you go to the store and buy them yourself, you are lucky that I am even giving you money." "I am doing what I want."

I awoke to somebody stroking my hair, opening my eyes, Cody was sitting on the side of the bed. He leaned in to gently kissed my lips, pretending to care he asking, "How are you feeling? I heard what happened." Sitting up quickly, I felt a sharp pain in my ribs, trying not to let him see me jump I stood up. "Wow, Brandy sure got you good, I do not know what you are doing to piss all these prostitutes off, but, whatever it is you better stop, or Faith is going after you." Retaliating quickly, "I charged Brandy." "What?" Cody asked, pushing me down on the bed, his pants fell to the floor, trying to slip his fingers in my panties, I slapped his hand away. Cody forced me to the bed, slid on top of me, whispered in my ear "There is something about you, I do not know what it is, but your eyes are beautiful." Closing my eyes, I turned my head when he tried to kiss my lips. He stood up quickly, I jumped up, his penis was fully erect, yanking my underwear off, pushing me back onto the bed, getting on top of me.

The only part of me that was not numb was my stomach, it felt nauseated. The sudden urge to get sick propelled me to the bathroom, locking the door behind me. When the sudden urge to get sick pasted I turned the shower on as hot as I could take it. I stood in the shower and washed myself, scraping the dirt off me, all I could think about were the prostitutes he was with. Screaming at the top of lungs "Ahhhh." I continued scraping my arms and I began to cry. There was a knock on the door, mom was asking, "What's going on in there?" Ignoring her I turned the shower off as I reached for my towel, I saw a different reflection in the mirror than the one months prior. The bruises on my face and ribs, my fat bloody lip, I could not stand it. I hated the girl looking back at me, quickly turning away from the reflection.

I went downstairs to take my pain killers, mom was sitting there with her fucking feet on the fucking table, having a fucking cigarette, and a coffee. She turned and looked at me and said, "What the fuck is wrong with you?" "Why are you screaming?" I calmly walked towards her, looking at her, my voice started to rise when I said, "What the fuck is wrong with me? What the fuck is wrong with you, are you fucking retarded?" "Do you know what you have done?" "She looked at me like she did not know what I was talking about, saying, "Me, I did not do anything, I don't do nothing." I wanted to slap her, yelling, "Maybe that is the fucking problem, you fucking do not do anything."

Storming back into the kitchen, I looked at the medication bottle, then back at mom, she just sat there, her back to me smoking her cigarette, feet still on the table. I took the bottle upstairs into the bathroom, locked the door. Still gripping the bottle in my hand, I slid down the wall and started to cry, opening the cap, I stood up and turned the water on. Emptying the bottle in my hand, looking at myself in the mirror, I thought, I could not stand what I saw. My face was black and blue, my lip was swollen with a cut with dry blood on it, it pained me to breathe. That mother fucker is not going away, my mother allows it, and I think enjoys it.

I threw all the pills in my mouth and tried to drink some water, except I could not get any water in my mouth, I started to gag instead. Running to the toilet I started to throw up. Collapsing on the floor in a ball, crying. Looking up saying "God why? Why? Why is this happening?" After I finished crying, I pulled myself up and stumbled into my room, packing my bag. I did not have much so it all fit. I flew down the stairs, putting my shoes on "Where are you going, when will you be home?" I glared at her, picking my bag up, slamming the door behind me.

I walked over to the Convenience store to get a pop. As I sat on the big rock at the bus stop to go to Tom's I kept looking over my shoulder. I said determined "God, this is silly, why am I the one who is scared, those strangers should be scared of you and what you can do." When I got to Tom's everybody was there, it was only a moment of humiliation when everybody looked over my injuries and was quickly replaced with a joint. It felt good being safe from Cody, If Cody knows where I am, he does not let on that he does.

Patricia, and Paige went home, Nancy, Bailey, and I stayed at Tom's and slept on the couch we talked half the night. When I woke up, I washed up and caught the bus to see Dr. Gere. He came in the room, looked at me shocked asking, "Goodness what happened to you?" Looking away ashamed I said, "I got beat up, but that isn't why I am here, I already saw the doctor for that." He had a sad look in his eyes asking, "What can I help you with?" "I would like a pregnancy test?" I blurted, His look became concerned when he asked, "How late are you?" I shrugged my shoulders saying, "I am not sure." He handed the requisition saying, "The lab is across the street, the results will take a couple of days, no news is good news." "Autumn, you take care." Ashamed I asked, "Could you please excuse me from school?" He scribbled on his notepad, tearing it off and handing it to me. Looking at it, I was excused for the whole week. Smiling I left.

standing at the mall doors I looked through the glass to see if it was safe to leave. I did not see Cody, Curtis, or Brandy, slowly I opened the door to get a better look, moving my eyes to the lab request to make it look like I was looking for an address, trying not to be so obvious that I was scared to leave. My stomach still hurting, my wheels set in motion as I moved, fear drove me forward. I walked quickly between the vehicles, through the parking lot to the bus terminal and got on the bus to Tom's. I did not want to be gone too long because everybody should be there by now, I did not want anybody to know my shame. I pulled the bell and walked to the back door of the bus. The doors opened, I stepped down and looked up saying, "God I know that I am not living for you right now, but I am trying, although I do not fully understand, I know you are going to be faithful as you always are."

Nobody asked any questions and I did not offer any information. The music playing was not gangster rap or R&B, I listened intently asking, "Who is this playing?" Bailey smiled saying, "Trooper here for a good time, Tom is tired of all that quote, "Rap shit." In his home. We poured ourselves drinks, sat down at the table, and started to roll a joint.

My stomach really hurt, keeling over I grabbed it, Nancy passed me the joint, I nodded my head no, saying, "I am not feeling well." As time went on my stomach-ache did not go away. I went to the washroom and realized I got my period, I never get cramps, it was heavy, I thought to myself, I guess this is what cramps feel like, whew, I am not pregnant. I went back downstairs saying to Nancy, "I am not feeling well I am going home." I grabbed my bag and left, going straight home to bed which is where I stayed most of the week.

Friday came and there was a dance, I was surprised when Cody showed up just before I was leaving, quickly I grabbed my things. Cody reached out and grabbed my arm drilling me saying, "You are a whore, look at you." My glance lingered as I looked at myself in the mirror, the thoughts about myself have not changed, I still hated the person in the mirror, the person he was trying to create. I yanked my arm back, looked at him like the words he said meant nothing, and left. Just because I felt horrible did not mean I had to act it; he was not going to get to me. God knew otherwise.

On the bus to meet Patricia and Nancy, permanent marker covered the seats. North Side Posse was written in big bold letters and then crossed out, sucks in bold letters, there were names of M.C gang members, girls making a public declaration of love. I kept reading until I got to the back of the bus to sit down, in big bold letters was written, AUTUMN MAYBERRY IS A FUCKING, DEAD WHORE. My heart stopped, fear and anxiety came over me. I quickly sat down and covered as much of the permanent marker as I could.

Patricia got on the bus with her walk man and sat down beside me, took her ear bud out and leaned in and looked at me and sang "My, my, my, my Prerogative." "I am so excited! It is going to be so much fun tonight." "Sean is going to be there." "Nancy is so excited." I smiled and said, "I have not met him yet." Patricia smiled saying, "This is going to be an awesome night. I tapped Patricia on the shoulder and moved as close to the window as I could so she would see the writing. Her green eyes grew big, her words were even bigger, "Who wrote that?" Annoyed with the question, I replied in a snotty voice, "I don't know." Patricia looked at me saying, "It was probably Brandy and you charged her so she will back off." I looked at her and said, "Yeah, you are right."

Nancy got on the bus; I showed her the writing. She looked at me saying, "Autumn what did you do?" firmly I flung, "I did not do anything, guilty by association." I knew it was either Brandy or Faith, but Cody was behind it all. However, Patricia and Nancy have not heard of Faith yet, so I slipped in, "Cody said that Faith is pissed off at me." Patricia asked, "Who is Faith?" I said, "Your guess is as good as mine, Cody said she is a prostitute and is after me, is it a coincidence?" "I do not care; I am having fun tonight." Nancy raised her arms and pulsed them saying, "That is right, fuck them, Woot Woot, Sean is going to be there tonight, he just got out of YOC." "YOC, what is that?" Inquisitively I asked, "Young Offenders Center." Nancy giggled.

Bailey, Paige, and Tammy were waiting for us when we arrived. We smoked a joint and quickly drank the Silent Sam on the way to the hall from the bus stop. We walked straight to the dance floor, Joan Jett I hate myself for loving you, was playing. Tammy danced liked she had no cares in the world. I knew that she had her struggles and has been through a lot, she just danced and said, "Fuck!"

Tammy and I went out for cigarette, holding each up as we laughed about the good time we were having. Tammy said that she was trying to forget that her foster family kicked her out. I offered "You could come stay with me." She was so excited when she said, "I will request it on Monday with my worker, your mom is awesome." We went back inside the hall just in time for Rumors by Club Nouveau to be playing. Nancy and Patricia, Paige, and Bailey were on the dance floor dancing, we danced our way to the group. The beat of the music overcame me, the words spoke to me. I tried not to think about the writing on the bus, I just wanted to forget, and have a good time. The words Cody said to me that were playing over and over in my head. I said to myself No, he is not going to break me, I am stronger.

The play list was great, Will Smith, Prince, Milli Vanilli, Madonna, Paula Abdul, slowly the music started to climax into N.W.A, Easy E. A couple of guys moved to the middle of the circle to dance, a brunette with jerry curls, and a red Adidas jacket and Levi's, and a blonde guy with a semi box cut, a black Adidas jacket, Levi's. I never saw them before. They started to break dance and hip hop. I noticed that they both had a red durag tucked into their back pockets. Then two black guys wearing all black with blue durags joined in, before I knew it there was a big circle surrounding us about ten to fifteen dancers, I have never seen anything like it. It was awesome they were having a dance off.

I felt a push from the left and I fell into Patricia and Nancy. Two black guys jumped on the two white boys. They started to fight. I was shocked and scared at the same time. The one black boy jumped the brunette while he was dancing. He did not see it coming as he fell to the floor, the black guy was on top of him smashing his head into the floor. Suddenly, his fist came up and started to punch the guy and somehow managed to get him off and end up on top and started to kick the shit out of him. The blonde guy saw it all coming and the guy did not stand a chance. Somebody yelled "COPS." The fight ended and everybody scattered, the music stopped, lights went on. We all met outside. The two white guys made their way to where we were standing. The brunette started to talk to Nancy. She had a concerned look on her face and moved in closer and said, "Are you OK?" "You are bleeding." He said, "Yeah I have to get out of here, I'll get arrested." He went in and gave Nancy a kiss and left with the blonde guy into the night.

We started to walk towards Tom's, I only assumed that was Sean Nancy was talking to, so I asked, "Why did those guys jump Sean and his friend?" Nancy said, "There is a rivalry between the two posse's and, they hate each other." I asked, "But why do they hate each other?" "I don't know." Nancy replied, "They are in gangs." I was confused, Nancy continued, "There will probably be a huge fight between the two posse's now that this happened."

CHAPTER 10

In Devin's Name

Monday morning at the bus terminal, Cody pulled up with Curtis, he got out of the car, walked directly to me, grabbing my arm, pulling me into the shelter. Once inside he pinned me up against the wall, stuck his tongue down my throat and started to dry hump me. I tried to get away from him, he whispered in my ear "What's the matter baby, don't you miss me?" "I need some money, give me some!" Turning my head, I used my back end against the wall to push him away from me, saying, "Get lost." Cody tried to schmooze me, "I have to go baby, give me some money." Determined I said, "No, I am not giving you money, I don't have any, remember, mom gave you all her money for drugs and booze for your party. I had to cover that." Cody grabbed me by my jacket and pulled me, his face met mine, using his other hand to dig in my pockets. He found some money, looked at it, held it up for me to see, saying, "Fucking bitch, quit lying to me." He put the money in his pocket and left me standing in the terminal.

I took a different bus after school and walked part of the way home, I took as spending time with God, also giving me time away from Cody. When I got home, I went straight upstairs and changed into my workout clothes, grabbing my library card, shoving it in my sock. Today is the day I could get the Paula Abdul VHS. I ran down the stairs, put my shoes on. Mom was sitting at her usual spot at the table asked, "Where are you going?" I grabbed a light jacket, ran out the door saying, "For a run."

The library was on the other side of the lake, it was a beautiful evening for a run. I was only allowed to take out the VHS once, so other people had the opportunity to borrow it as well. Excitement overtook me, my legs pushed me faster, walking right up to the shelf where the VHS should be, it was not there. I proceeded to the front desk where the librarian was, asking, "Excuse me, could you please tell me if the Paula Abdul VHS is in?" She smiled at me and started to walk to the side counter saying, "It was just returned." I smiled asking, "Am I able to take it out?" She replied "Yes, there is nobody on the list." I smiled and passed her my library card and said, "Thank you." Took the VHS and ran home, walked straight downstairs and put the VHS in the player.

I grabbed my well-worn capezio's, slipped them on, tied a knot in the front of my t-shirt and started to stretch. I love dancing, excited to finally have the VHS, I grabbed it and put it in the player saying, "Because Cody is the snake." Pushing play, I did my warmups across the floor, looking at myself in the strategically placed mirrors hanging on nails from the boards, of the unfinished basement.

I stayed downstairs dancing for hours, Cold Hearted Snake was definitely my favorite, Cody being the snake, my body felt every beat, like the venom of the snake's bite. It was a lot of fun pretending that I was part of the troupe, the moves that I could not see I would choreograph myself. I caught a glimpse through the corner of my eye, Cody was standing there watching me. He looked surprised when he asked, "What are you doing?" "Is that what all the mirrors are for?" I quickly went to turn the music off, all sweaty, I looked away embarrassed saying, "Nothing."

Quickly I went upstairs and turned the shower on and went into my bedroom to get my torn-up pajamas. I turned around and Cody scared me, he was standing there. I must have looked annoyed because he grabbed my arm and said, "Don't look at me like that, you better watch it." He grabbed the front of my sweatpants and pulled them to see if I still had my period. They snapped back and he said, "You should be done by now." I snapped around, went into the bathroom, locked the bathroom door, and got into the shower.

When I got out of the shower and went downstairs to get something to eat. Cody was not there. "Where is Cody?" I asked mom, "He left but said he will call later." She said. I rolled my eyes and went into the kitchen to make something to eat. There was nothing so I went into my room, got down on my knees and started to pray. I prayed the Lord's prayer, (Matthew 6:9-13) Then I started to worship the Lord, my tears flowed freely, "Please deliver me from this, help me understand why you are allowing this, help me understand mom, help me forgive her for putting me in this situation, Please keep me safe and healthy." "God, I feel so good and free from everything when I dance and run, I am close to you, please open a door for me to become a dancer. This I ask in your name Amen."

Lying in bed the doorbell rang. I thought to myself, that is weird, who could that be? Hesitantly I got up and answered the door and it was Devin. I was surprised. Devin was a tall, skinny black guy with pimples all over his face and neck. He had a box cut and resembled Bobby Brown in puberty. I have seen him around a lot, but I never talk to him. He said, "Cody told me to meet him here." I said, "Cody isn't here yet, you can just wait here at the table for him." I turned away, went upstairs to bed.

I was almost asleep when I noticed my bedroom door open and the light from the hallway revealed a black silhouette in the doorway. I sat up and I thought it was Cody at first, but he was not built like Cody he was a lot skinnier. It was Devin, he walked towards me and sat on the end of the bed and looked at me. I said, "Get out, Cody isn't here, I am trying to sleep go wait downstairs." I turned over and pulled the covers back over my shoulder.

Devin moved and I thought that he was going to leave so I waited for the door to open but it did not. Instead he slid up behind me, so I moved over and turned over on my stomach. Devin put his leg over me and rubbed up against me, whispering in my ear, "You are so hot, let me fuck you." Shutting him down, "NO." "Did Cody put you up to this?" I tried to get up, but Devin moved and put all his weight on me. Devin continued to whisper, "Cody will never know." I said "NO!"

I tried, but I could not move, Devin whispered, "You make me so hot, Please, Cody will never know." I said firmly "No, not happening, leave now, I will tell Cody." Devin ran his hand down my side and grabbed the right cheek of my ass." saying, "You have a nice body, I think about fucking you every time I see you, Please!" I quickly responded "No." I tightened my thighs together. Devin said, "I like a girl that has strong thighs." He pulled my pants down and forced my legs apart and shoved his fingers up my vagina and gave a couple of forceful pushes, he pulled his fingers out and got off me. I turned over and looked at him, He lifted his hand and smelled his fingers and said "Bitch, you are nothing but a hoe." He quietly opened the door and left. I closed my eyes pleading, "God, I know you are there!" Why are you allowing this?" My tears flowed and whisked me off to sleep.

My head hurt in the morning trying to determine if it was a dream last night. Devin could not have; it was so real. I pulled the covers back over my head wanting the world to go away. My heart was heavy, my stomach hurt, and the tears started to fall to my pillow. I started to pray. "God, I love you, take my tears and form an ocean, wash me away into your loving arms, protect me from my enemies. Amen"

Leaving for work mom was downstairs sitting at the kitchen table, her feet up, having a coffee and cigarette. "Good morning!" I said, pretending to be sincere. She took a drag of her cigarette her face was expressionless. Looking in the fridge like something might have changed from last night, and there was nothing, I thought, I will eat at work. I walked over to the table and picked up the pack of cigarettes and opened the pack. It had about five in it, I dropped the pack on the table and put on my shoes. Mom said. "Pick me up some coffee and cigarettes." As the door closed.

My feet hesitantly carried me to the back of bus, anticipating cruel and scary things written about me. Kiss 'N' Cee, written in bold letters, scribbled beside it was, Autumn Mayberry is a fucking dead HOE!!!" I turned and sat down directly on seat, looking out the window. I whispered, "God, I know you hear my plea, please end this. Whining, I am so tired, please God, help me, deliver me." My hands fell to my lap, closed my eyes, and started to worship.

When I opened my eyes, my attention was drawn to the all the things that God created, it made my heart happy, who could not help but smile. The pine trees up ahead hid the convenience store by Nancy's house, the details in the tiniest living cells could only be created by God. Suddenly I felt like I was slapped in the face. I pulled the bell, grabbed my bag. The bus came to a halt, I stumbled to the back doors, they flew open and I sprinted over to get a better look.

Shocked, I stood there and stared at the power box spray painted black, "AUTUMN MAYBERRY IS A DEVIN ANDERSON FUCKER!!!" The tears started to fill my eyes, my legs felt weak and my stomach started to cramp. I took a deep breath in, lifted my head high to the sky and whispered, "Don't cry, don't cry." Looking around to see if Cody was close by, there was no sign of him or Curtis's car. Walking with a blow to the stomach into the convenience store, straight to the counter meekly asking, "Can I please get a pack of Du Maurier light regular?" As I reached over to grab a lighter out of the neatly lined up lighters and placed it on the counter for the cashier to see. I dug frantically for the money out of my bag, paid for the cigarettes and lighter and left.

I took the wrapping off the pack of cigarettes, pulled a cigarette out, put the pack in my bag, and lit the cigarette, and walked back to the bus stop. Feeling confused looking at the power box from a distance, the writing playing a game with my mind. I inhaled my cigarette, I did not know what else to do, I trust God, I pray, and I spend time with him, why was this happening? I heard the bus coming, I threw my cigarette to the ground, stepped on it and defeatedly got on the bus, sitting quietly looking out the window on my way to work trying to fight back my tears.

After work, the girls and I walked over to seven eleven to get some hash from Kaleb. Kaleb seemed high already and was very convincing when he said, "This is some good shit!" That was just what I needed, while digging in my bag I asked Kaleb, "Can I get a gram?" He took the money and pulled a baggie out of his inside pocket and handed it to me. Taking it proudly saying, "Thank you."

The music was playing, the knives were heating up at Tom's while we sat at the kitchen table rolling a joint. I sat across the table looking at Paige wondering if she thought it was funny when Brandy kicked my ass? I wanted to know, Instead I decided I was just going to enjoy the evening, Paige was only fourteen years old.

The doorbell rang and Tom answered the door, it was Dakota and Luc. I rolled my eyes and thought this is not going to be fun, who invited them? They walked straight to the kitchen with a swag in their walk like they were so important. They immediately joined in doing blades and smoking the joint. Dakota choked back coughing, looking at me saying, "Autumn, does Cody know you are here?" I just looked at him and thought they spoil everything. I grabbed my bag, leaned towards Nancy, and quietly said, "I am going to go, call me later."

It was a nice night for a walk, the stars were twinkling in the deep blue evening sky, they dropped down to the earth to light my way. The universe became my dance partner as I danced from star to star, nothing mattered yet it was everything. Reaching for the stars and holding them in my hands brought hopes of the promises of tomorrow and God's unending love for me. I sang,

"God has got me, God has got me" Running up the stairs, through the front door.

Oh yeah this is reality, dishes were not washed, and the house was a mess. Mom was walking the floor, she looked at me in panic state, asking, "Do you have any smokes?" As high as I was, my anger towards her disappeared and was replaced with concern. I felt bad for her, she worried a lot. I just did not understand her. It has been an awfully long time since she has said, I love you, she does not seem to want happiness for me, I wondered why she would let Cody take the one gift, that I could give to only one. I pulled the cigarettes out of my bag and handed them to her. She did not even say thank you. I went upstairs, changed into my work out clothes, grabbed my bag and came back downstairs. I opened the pack of cigarettes and took one out and went down to the basement.

I sat down, opened my bible, to begin reading the scriptures. Opening it directly to the Song of Solomon, I started to cry, "God I don't understand, you knew I wanted to be a virgin on my wedding night, I was supposed to be my beloved's and he would be mine. I was never going to experience choosing." I wiped my tears and ripped the page out of my bible, then strategically ripped a rectangular piece off the page, I reached over to my bag and took the hash out, broke a piece off, I grabbed my safety pin from the inside of my shirt. I placed the piece of hash on the end of the pin, then used my lighter to warm it up. I started to crumble it onto the paper. Taking the cigarette, ripping a piece off the bottom, mixed it together, put the mixture of hash and tobacco on the rectangular piece of paper, then rolled it into a joint. I licked the whole joint and tore a long thin strip off the last cardboard page of my bible, rolled it up and pushed down the tobacco to fit in the filter. I had too much paper, so I took a piece off and fit the filter in perfectly. I thought of Kaleb when he said, "This is some good shit." I could not help but laugh as I said, "Yep this is good shit."

My heart jumped when mom yelled, "Autumn did you get coffee?" I went upstairs and said "No." Looked at the time and quickly ran out the door to the store. There was a young boy about ten with dark hair and big blue eyes behind the counter. Quickly I grabbed a pound of Nabob coffee and went up to the counter and paid, smiling I said, "Thank you." I leaned against wall outside the store, lit my joint and took a deep breath in and continued to walk home. Only smoking half the joint.

Putting the coffee on the table at mom's feet. She said, "Make me a coffee." I looked at her, kissed my teeth, said "No." Went downstairs, pushed play on the ghetto blaster, slipped on my capezio's and started jazz walks across the floor, practicing my spotting. Madonna like a prayer was playing. I noticed that Cody had a bag of his belongings on the bed, so I picked it up and shoved it under the bed and went back to warmups. Keep it together started to play and I stopped my warmup and began to lip sync and do hip hop and jazz that I have picked up watching the video. "Autumn." Mom yelled. I changed the music to Holiday by Madonna and acted like I did not hear her.

After the tape played, I went and turned the VHS on with Paula Abdul, Cold hearted snake. I danced for hours. I practiced jumps, leaps, and pirouettes. I started to stretch, feeling bad for rolling a joint with the bible, sadly I said, "God please forgive me, forgive me for getting high and using your word to smoke it." "Please get me through this, I am so tired, and I need you right now." "Why aren't you hearing my cries?" "Please make Cody stop." "Thank you for giving me a job, thank you that I am able to work." Thank you for the body that I am able to dance and worship you with." "God please heal my stomachache, this I ask in your name, Amen."

It was getting late and mom still had not cleaned up at all, she had four coffee cups lined up on the table. The ashtray had butts falling over the edges because she would light a cigarette and let them burn. I put my jacket and shoes on, walked over to the park, sat on the swing, smoking the other half of my joint, then flushed the butt down the toilet to get rid of the evidence. I stayed up most of the night cleaning the house, I could see the morning sun coming up when I finally went to bed.

Cody has not been around, the rumors of Faith looking for me were going around like a hot potato. I was really scared, the feeling of anxiety followed me around. Who is Faith? I did not know who was, or what she looked like, I am not going to even see it coming. Nobody knows who she was. Cody said she is a prostitute and that I made her angry. My hope was she was going to leave me alone because of the charges against Brandy.

By the end of the week Cody did show up at the bus terminal. He came up from behind, grabbed me and kept walking. He whispered in my ear "What the hell are you doing here?" "Faith is coming, and you better get out of here." I started to resist Cody as he pushed me from behind. My heart was beating out of my chest and I thought somebody would see my distress and hopefully help me, nobody did. Cody stopped and looked at me and said, "What are you doing, do you want Faith to fucking kill you?"

Frantically I looked around at the buses in the terminal to see which bus would take me closest to home. I saw a bus and quickly walked to it. Cody followed me and said "What are you doing? Faith is coming and I am trying to save you, I am trying to help you." The bus closed its doors I reached out and banged on the door and the bus driver opened the door, quickly I hopped on the bus and heard the doors close behind me. Looking back Cody was standing at the bus stop. I showed the bus driver my bus pass and found an empty seat as I watched Cody walk back over to where everybody was standing.

I started breathing in deeply to stop my stomach pains, the bus speed off in the opposite direction. The feeling of being chased did not dissipate. When the bus stopped, and I got off my eyes wondered in every direction looking to see if Curtis was lurking in the background. My stomach cramped causing me to crouch over as I wailed "Ouch," Taking a deep breath in stammering, "You'll be OK." I took another look around and headed home. What should have taken only ten minutes took me twice as long because my stomach kept cramping.

Cody had me so scared, it was really affecting me. The thought of spending time with God in my pajamas for the next couple of days was comforting. The reflection in the mirror said it all, my tattered pajamas hung off my body like rags. Feeling broken, used, and unworthy for my future husband. I sighed, quickly turned off the light and jumped on my bed, scared of the monsters that may be hiding below. I pulled the quilt over my head, closed my eyes feeling God's hands pick me up and hold me. Cuddling in with my pillows whispering, "Good night God, I love you."

CHAPTER 11
Faith

My body and spirit tired, sleeping snug in bed was the only time, and place, that there was peace, comfort, and no pain. That is where I stayed for a couple of days. Mom must have had enough of my sleeping, "Get out of bed you fucking whore, get your ass to school before I fucking beat you." She screamed as she flipped my bed over. Lying on the floor still unsure what just happened, I retorted "For somebody who can't do anything for herself, she finds the strength to flip my bed, I HATE HER."

Instead of going to school I went to work and picked up my pay cheque, stopped at the bank to cashed it, folded the money in a piece of paper and tucked it in my bag and started to walk home. My heart opened and my lips stared moving, "God you are my heavenly father, you made me, you love me, you want good for me, what the enemy intends for my harm you intend for my good." before I knew it I was almost running, I put my bag on my back and completed the race.

I got home and my legs were like jelly and I had sweat dripping off my forehead. I went straight downstairs to stretch and I picked up praying where I left off, it quickly turned into pleading with God, begging God to end this whole ordeal with Cody, I was on my knees asking "God are you punishing me?" "What possibly could I have done to deserve this?" "God, my heart is heavy, my stomach sore with anxiety, my feet still choose to dance before you. Thank you that I still have dance, with that I will worship you." I took my capezio's out and held them up and said, "Even if the soles wear out, I will dance for you." Slipping on my shoes I started my jazz walks and spotting.

My attention was drawn to Cody's bag. I walked over to the bed, pulled it out from underneath, placing it on the bed and opened it. There was a black t-shirt, and under the shirt was a book. I pulled it out, it was a yearbook, on the front it had blue metallic bold letters Most High College, and in the same blue it said class of eighty-five. I open the book and started to read the writing inside. Cody it has been great getting to know you, Cody you are an amazing person, I am going to miss you Cody, I know that you are going to be successful. I started to flip through the pages. Cody was in some of the pictures, I could not say anything, I sat down on the bed, closed the yearbook.

I grabbed the bag to see what else was in it, pulling out a little black book that read British Passport. Inside a picture of a young black boy, the name read Cody Ethan Erickson, Date of birth Feb eighteenth, nineteen sixty. Studying the photo, it was a young Cody, doing the math in my head, that made Cody twenty-eight years old. I could have sworn that my heart stopped beating. Cody confesses to be a Christian. I had no ideal he went to a Christian College. I knew that Cody befriended all my friends, why did he lie about his age? I wanted to vomit; a twenty-eight-year-old, Christian man is having his way with me. I am sixteen, I questioned out loud, "What does he want with me?" Shoving the yearbook and t-shirt back in the bag and kicking it under the bed. I took the passport and went up to my bedroom, pulled the chair over to my closet. Moved the clothes aside, shoving the passport in the far back corner, pushing the clothes back over to hide it.

I jumped when the phone rang, I heard mom answer it. When I went downstairs mom hung up the phone, clapped her hands together, looked at me and said, "That was Tammy's worker, I am approved, Tammy can move in next week." Walking into the kitchen my sarcasm blurted out, "I am surprised that they approved you." Mom looked shocked, I firmly looked at her and said "You are selfish, all you care about is having your coffee and cigarettes. If you don't have your cigarettes you hit." I could feel my anger starting to rise. "We never have any food, and you put your own children in danger." Mom stood up, came at me, grabbed my hair with her left hand and slapped me. I tried to pry her hand away from my head, but once her hand has grip there is no getting loose. She shook my head then let go, going to sit back down at the table. I shot arrows at her, yelling, "I HATE YOU!"

I stormed out of the kitchen and went back downstairs. I ripped another piece of the paper off that I previously tore out of the bible and rolled a joint, went upstairs and left. I started walking and I ended up at Patricia's. I stopped and rang the doorbell and a lady in her thirties answered the door, she looked like an older version of Patricia. I ask, "Is Patricia home?" She said, "No she went out." I said "OK, just tell her that Autumn stopped in." She said "OK, I will." I knew she would not be home, but I thought that I would try, home was not an option right now.

I made my way to the Lake, sat on the bench, staring at the partially frozen water. The events with Cody played through my mind, I wanted to cry but could not. I knew that I was in danger, but I could not piece everything together. The sharp pains in my stomach started up again, I leaned over and started to take deep breaths in. The pain slowly went away, and my anxiety was making my heartbeat fast. I looked up to the sky and it was starting to get dark. My eyes started to tear up as I prayed, "God thank you for your holy spirit that lead me to look into Cody's bag." "Please God keep me safe, remove Cody from my life."

Reaching into my pocket I took the lighter and joint out, looking around to see if anyone was coming, a couple with their golden retriever were walking towards me. Quickly slipping the joint back in my pocket and waited. As they got closer the dog started to pull and wanted to say hello. I smiled, looked at the couple and asked, "May I pet your dog?" They smiled and said "Sure." I massaged behind his ears, then did a full body rub and said, "Aren't you just a sweetheart." It was relaxing, the dog started to lick my face and the guy pulled the leash and said, "That's enough, let's go." They continued their walk and disappeared in the distance. I waited, took the joint back out of my pocket. The coast was clear, so I lit the joint and inhaled deeply, saying, "God please forgive me for getting high, my body is a temple, this is only temporary. Just get me through this."

It was a sleepless night, Cody being twenty-eight and the events of the last eight months replayed in my mind. Finally sleep found me for an hour before it was time to get up and go to work. I cried, "Ugh, I need sleep, I don't want to go to work today." Pulling the blankets back up over my head and fell back to sleep. New kids on the block, you got the right stuff was playing on the radio when my eyes finally opened. Mom told work I was sick when they called.

Cody interrupted my workout; I did not see him standing there at first. I was kind of taken back because he has not been around for a while, wanting to get away I went for the stairs, he moved so he would block my path. I moved to go to the other side, he moved there as well, calmly asking, "Where do you think you are going?" Urgently I replied, "Upstairs." Cody gently placed my hand in his, led me the ghetto blaster, gently saying, "I got something to show you." Cody reached in his pocket, held up a tape, took the tape out, replaced it with the one he had in his pocket, and pressed play.

The music started, I did not recognize it, I continued to listen, it was not familiar. It was soft and slow; after listening to it for a moment, I knew I have never heard it before. Cody started to move his feet from side to side, then added his hips slowly, subtly put in a soft hip pop. Cody started to take his top off to the music. I turned to go upstairs, he grabbed me and said, "I am trying to show you something, why do you have to be a bitch all the time?" As he gently ran his hands up and down my body, he whispered in my ear the lyrics of the song. "I can tell you how I feel about you night and day, I love you in the rain or shine, and making love in the rain is fine." He stepped back and finished taking the rest of his clothes off.

I turned my head, Cody used his hand to move my chin, so I was looking at him, slowly as he moved towards me. His manly parts touching me. The next song started, he sang "Rescue me, Do you wanna, do you wanna wanna, there is a girl standing there made just for me," He moved towards the bed and laid me down on the bed and pulled my clothes off and got on top of me. Cody continued to sing, "If I'm not your lover, if I'm not your friend, just tell me baby just what I am." The music stopped, I crawled over Cody, he grabbed me, pulling me back down saying, "No, stay here, this is where it happened the first time." I looked at him saying, "Yeah, I remember."

I fell asleep, waking up beside Cody, he was still sleeping. I watched him sleep for a while, he had nice skin, he had hair product in his hair that made his curls smooth and perfectly defined. I could see a few tiny little curls on his chest. I slid out of the bed slowly, and quietly, so I did not wake him, had a shower, and went to sleep in my bed. In the morning Cody was gone. The phone rang and it was Patricia on the other end asking, "Do you want to go the mall with me?" "Nancy, Bailey, and Paige are going to be there, I need to buy some makeup." I said "Yeah, I just need to get ready, if I don't see you on the bus, I will meet you in the food court."

Patricia pulled her compact out purse to check her makeup, seeing the reflection, she giggled, "I really needed new make-up, look." Showing us the broken mirror, and almost empty cover-up, placing it back in her purse, moving onto the new things she purchased. She grabbed her bag, opened it, showing us the fun things, she bought, explaining what it was for and how she would use it. Patricia put everything back in the bag and shoved it in her purse saying, "Make-up is expensive." "I watched my baby brother last night so I could earn some money to buy makeup. Guess who came by my house when my parents were out." We were all looking, listening, wondering if she was going to tell us. She had a look of horror on her face saying, "Luc, he was extremely high; he was tripping out. He had a machete!" Wondering who carries a machete, I repeated, "A machete?" Patricia opened her arms about two and a half feet saying, "A big knife." "I told him to get rid of it, but he wouldn't." Patricia's eyes grew bigger, she leaned in to talk, so we all leaned forward to listen carefully. "Do you want to know what he did?" We listened intently, "He tried giving the machete to my baby brother to hold, I quickly grabbed it away telling him that he had to leave, that my parents are going to be home any minute." "Luc wouldn't leave, I was really scared." "My parents would have killed me if they saw that." I shivered saying, "They are all scary." Bailey quickly added, "Tom doesn't like them coming over to the house." Paige agreed. Nancy said, "They are doing some nasty stuff." The table grew quiet. Patricia, Bailey, and Paige were looking directly behind me and Nancy, Patricia nodded her head as if to say, somebody was coming.

Nancy and I turned and looked, Dakota and Luc were walking into the food court. Dakota was doing a gangster walk and Luc looked paranoid. Dakota came up behind me, kicked the bottom of my seat and asked "Autumn, do you have any money?" I kind of jumped, my heart racing trying not to let them see I was scared and replied "No." Dakota leaned in and said, "Don't lie to me." I said, "I am not." He leaned in to face me and said "Bitch give me some money before I beat the shit out of you. "Nancy quickly said "I have two dollars." She went into her purse and handed it to Dakota. Dakota said, "Thank you." He grabbed me by the back of my hair and said, "You are lucky bitch." and pushed my head forward. Luc started laughing and said, "Yeah Bitch, you are lucky." They walked up to order something in the food court. Embarrassed and scared I stood up saying, "I am going to go." I quickly walked to the escalator watching my back as I went down.

I was waiting for my bus for what felt like forever, suddenly I heard, "There you are, I have been looking for you." Cody pulled me in giving me a sloppy kiss, releasing saying, "Who said that you could go out." My heart still racing from what just happened with Dakota said. My head was starting to spin when I heard, "Autumn." I was a little relieved to see Lisa standing there. Cody whispered a threat in my ear. "You better get on the bus." Lisa looked concerned, I went and gave her a hug asking, "What are you doing here?" She said, "I am worried about you, what is going on?" I did not tell her, but I was scared. "I said "Nothing." "I don't hear from you and you are never at school. Tell me what is going on, right now." Lisa demanded, from behind I heard Cody say, "Autumn, the bus is here." I turned and looked, Cody was standing at the door and got on. Lisa pulled me so I would look at her, begging, "Autumn, don't go with him." I looked at Cody then back at Lisa saying, "I am sorry." I pulled away and got on the bus. The bus ride home was quiet, I sat in the back seat looking out the window.

When we got to the house, I played Sega volleyball, not very well either, it took everything I had not to confront Cody about his age. Then he would know that I went through his things, and that his passport was no longer there. Even though I felt closer to the girls, I have not told them Cody's real age. Cody leaned over smacking my lips with a kiss saying, "Somebody is picking me up, we have something we have to do." I continued to play Sega saying, "Oh." I did not ask too many questions because I really did not care. Cody put on his jacket and shoes and left.

A few minutes later the doorbell rang, I was shocked, yet happy to see Dan, he stood at the bottom of the stairs with a half-smile saying, "Hi Autumn." Still surprised I said, "Hi." Then leaned in and gave him a hug. He politely asked, "I hope you don't mind that I came here today, can you go for a walk?" I nodded my head saying, "Sure, come in while I put my shoes on." Dan said, "I will just wait here." I quickly slipped my shoes on, closing the door behind me, running down the stairs. I looked at Dan smiling, saying, "it is good to see you, how are things." Dan said, "Good, really good, I have a new job in a warehouse, and I make twenty dollars an hour." "Mom finally dumped that bum." Changing the subject back to me he asked, "How are things with you?" "I never hear from you anymore, is everything OK?" I nodded my head saying, "Things are fine." I felt the tears starting to fill my eyes. Dan said, "What's wrong?" I said, "Mom stuff, you know." Dan did not look convinced when asked, "Do you need some money?" I shook my head no, he continued, "Do you need a place to stay?" "I am sure mom would let you stay with us if you needed to." I said, "No that's fine, let's talk about something else."

We walked for a while and it was nice to be around somebody and not look over my shoulder or be scared. We headed back in the direction of my house, I asked, "How did you get here?". He replied, "I caught the bus." I said, "I will walk you to the bus stop." Dan shook his head no, saying, "Nah, I am going to walk home." "That is far." I blurted, "lots of time to think." Dan said, I gave Dan a hug saying, "It was nice seeing you, thanks for coming." He looked at me and asked, "Are you sure there is nothing you want to tell me?" I nodded and said "Yeah." He gave me another hug and said, "Don't be a stranger." I smiled and smiled, "Ok."

I could hear faint music when I walked in the house, Cody was already home, he was in the living room playing music. I went into the kitchen to make something to eat, Cody came dancing into the kitchen, pulling me into the living room as he lip-sang Oran

Juice Jones, The Rain, "I saw you and him walking in the rain, you were holding hands and I will never be the same." Confused, I wondered, did he follow me when I went for a walk with Dan. We were not holding hands; we have been friends for a couple of years. Not getting sleep at night has become a regular thing since Cody came around, I laid awake most of the night.

Science class the teacher looked at me saying, "Autumn you are no longer in this class." I went down to the office, I was officially kicked out of school, too many absences. I went to my locker, got my books, and caught the bus to hang out at Tom's. Nancy, Patricia, Bailey, and Paige were there with me and we were doing blades. The front door opened, we heard, "What the hell is going on here?" we turned and there was a tall indigenous lady coming down the hallway. We panicked and dashed out the back door, down the alley. We stopped and looked at Bailey. Patricia asked, "Who is that?" Bailey said, "Tom's mom." Nancy was laughing and managed to ask, "Oh no is he going to be in trouble?' "We left everything there." Bailey said "I will call him from my parents house, they are not home right now.

We all walked over to Bailey's house, she dialed Tom's phone number, we all leaned into the receiver, trying to hear what is going to be said. Bailey held the phone out saying, "Hello, do you mind, I cannot hear." Only backing a little, we tried to listen to as much of the conversation as we could. Bailey hung up the phone saying, "His mom is pissed!" "She picked up the plate and threw it against the wall, there is a hole in the wall and the plate shattered, they are grounded for a while." We were all a little scared, probably good we just went home.

While in a deep sleep I awoke to someone sliding up next to me. At first, I thought I was dreaming, then I thought Cody, I opened my eyes and had to take a second look because it was George. George was a Milano boy, hazel eyes, his hair light brown with a box cut. He always wore a green army jacket, and Levi's blue jeans. I never talked to him because he was dating a girl at our school named Anna. Anna's locker was right across from my locker. She would fight any girl that even looked at him.

"What the heck are you doing?" I asked, George whispered "SSH, it is OK." I moved quickly, trying to jump out of bed, George swung his right leg over me, using his body weight to push himself, so I was on my back and he was on top of me. His hands pinning my arms down, saying, "SSH, it is OK." George gently kissed my lips, moving just enough to be able to take my panties off, I could feel his manness against my body. He maneuvered himself between my legs, I was frozen. George whispered, "You are so beautiful, my cock is hard for you, come on baby tell me you like it." I did not see this coming, still unable to move, I could not cry, I could not scream. When he was done, he gently kissed me again asking, "Don't you like that?" He rolled off me, wrapping his arm and legs around me so I could not move.

My eye's focused on the ceiling, my heart hurt, feeling cold as I shivered. The coolness circulating through my body like the icy winds slowly freezing the streams. My eyes closing like I was going into hibernation, hoping when I awoke that the early spring morning will bring new dreams of hope and melt the darkness away.

Morning came, I stretched and took a deep breath in, thinking was that a dream last night? Closings my eyes while throwing my arm across the bed to feel if my bed was empty. George was not there. Sitting up quickly, looking around the room to see if anything was different from the time I went to bed until now. I reached for the crumpled paper on my bed, it was twenty dollars. Quietly I whimpered, "I am not a prostitute, men just can't come and go as they like." Dropping the crumpled paper on the floor.

Storming into the bathroom to turn the shower on so the filth can be washed from my body. Slowly adjusting the temperature hotter and hotter until it caused me to fall to my knees in pain, crying, "God, please help me now, please make it stop. Do you not see my pain?" "I am sorry for saying that there was only one worthy of being with me, that I was only going to be with one, is that why I am going through this?" "God please don't make me go through this anymore, God please, please, make it stop." I curled up in the fetal position, crying until the water started to run warm, the cooling water was feeling just as painful. Standing up to turn the water off, not wanting to get out of the shower, knowing that the reflection in mirror was beyond recognition, far away and foggy. Sliding down the bathroom wall in disbelief, a tear rolling down my cheek.

Mom was downstairs, the only thing I felt was anger, and hatred, towards her, it was written on my face, she asked me, "What's wrong?" I asked mom "Did you let George in?" She looked at me and said, "Yeah he came early this morning, said that Cody told him to come here." I loudly said, "Cody is not here, do you even know his name?" Mom said, "NO, He was supposed to meet Cody." My eyes piercing at her, yelling, "What the fuck is wrong with you?" Mom showed no emotions, like it was no big deal when she said, "What did I do, I did not do anything." I stood there puzzled trying to read what possibly is making her think the way she does, firmly saying, "You did not do anything?" "I hate you! I HATE YOU, no, I fucking hate, your stupid ass." Running upstairs, I stopped halfway up because mom asked, "Do you have money for some smokes?" Stomping up the rest of stairs, grabbing the crumpled-up money off the floor. Enjoying the moment when I threw the money in her face, saying, "Money is money even if it is dirty. Do you even know how I got that?" Mom turned her head, looked away like I was not even standing there. There were so many emotions flowing through me. I felt shame, I felt anger, I felt alone, I wanted to die. I stood there looking at Mom. She looked at me through the corner of her eye, puckered up her lips, pulled out a cigarette, slowly brought it to her lips, lit the cigarette, took a long drag, and then blew the smoke out.

Mom has not been the same since our family was reunited, she did not care. I left to meet Nancy and Patricia on the bus. Bailey and Paige were at the bus terminal when we got there. We walked over to the mall and sat down in the parkade, smoking a joint. A security vehicle started to approach us. Nancy quickly threw the joint and we walked up to the food court. Intense anxiety came over me, I could not help but look over my shoulder, I asked the girls, "Can we go?" "I am scared." Nancy said, "Where are we going to go?" "We can't go to Tom's." My heart was racing, hoping to convince them I added, "What if Dakota comes, or Faith?" Nancy replied, "You are having a bad trip, just relax." I took a deep breath in, sighing, "Easy for you to say, you are not going to get your ass kicked everywhere you go, I do not think you understand, my stomach hurts."

The mall was busy with a lot of teenagers not in school, I felt unsafe, Faith could easily come out of the crowd and attack me, my feeling ware legitimate. I stopped looking around, whispering over Nancy's shoulder, "Did you know that Cody is twenty-eight?" Nancy whipped her head looking at me shocked, "What, no way." I continued "I found a bag of Cody's stuff in the basement; I didn't look at it for a long time." "It has his yearbook, passport and a few other things. He is from London." "His date of birth is Feb eighteenth, nineteen sixty."

Nancy was shocked, raising her voice just enough to get the attention of everybody at the table, "Get out." Nancy turned so they could all hear, "Cody is twenty-eight." Affirming, "I am not having a bad trip, nothing is right about Cody, and what I am going through, Cody is getting these prostitutes after me, I want to leave." Nancy said nervously "OK." We all got up and walked over to the bus terminal. Bailey said, "We can ride the buses." So, we did, through downtown, then through subdivisions where Bailey, and Paige got off because it was close to Paige's house.

We got off the bus at the terminal and started to walk to our bus stop. Through the corner of my eye there was a tall black girl with a tight tube dress run from the parking lot to catch her bus. I heard, "There you are you fucking bitch." She jumped on the curb, slapping me in the face, grabbing my bag and started to go through it. Unsure of what was happening I looked up to see my surroundings. Cody was standing beside Curtis's car, watching the event. She asked, "where is your money?" I stuttered, "I do not have any money." Angrily she said, "Don't lie to me bitch." Her hand came up, she grabbed my hair, yanked my head, let got and slapped me in the face again, took one last look in my bag and proudly walked over to where Cody was standing. They stood there talking for a moment, then got in the car and drove off.

Patricia and Nancy walked towards me asking, "Are you OK?" I said "Yeah." Still shaking I thought that was not so bad. I went through my bag, opening the folded piece of paper and looked, my money was still in there. I had a couple of hundred dollars that I have been saving, I did not dare leave it at home, mom goes through my things and would steal it.

I sat there quietly looking out the window on the bus ride home. Patricia asked, "What happened?" Describing to them "Faith was going through my bag looking for money." I reached in my bag and pulled out the folded piece of paper and said, "Guess that is why she is a fucking dumb hoe, she didn't find the money." Making my way to the bus doors to get off at my stop, Patricia asked, "Are you going to be OK walking home?" "I said "I do not know." I got off the bus and threw my bag over my shoulder and ran home as fast as I could.

I walked in the door and there was music playing that I never heard before. A tall skinny indigenous man was sitting at the table, his long legs almost reached to the other side of the table. Mom said, "Autumn this is Brent, I used to babysit him when he was little." "He just moved here and does not know anybody." He smiled and said "Hello." I said 'Hi." I made myself a coffee and sat down at the table. The music was catchy, and I really like it, so I asked, "Who is this playing?" He smiled saying, "Only the greatest band ever, Tragically Hip." I asked, "What is the name of this song?" He smiled and said, "Boots or Hearts." I said, "I like it."

Mom announced, "Tammy is moving in tomorrow." "Guess what else?" Annoyed I looked at her, snapping, "What?" Mom blurted, "The Police called today." That got my attention, intrigued I made eye contact with her, asking, "What for?" She said "Dave's guns got stolen from the house. Luc and another guy got stopped by police, they found the guns on them." My first thought was that party mom threw. I asked, "Does Dave know?" She said, "Yeah the police called the army base and notified Dave." I inquired, "Is Dave mad?" She said, "He was upset, just glad nobody was hurt, or no criminal offense was committed." I looked at Brent and said, "It was nice to meet you, I am going for a run." "Will you be coming by again?" He smiled and said "Yes, nice to meet you as well."

On my run my eyes kept checking my surroundings like I was in a battle zone, my legs carrying me as fast as they could. My stomach started to hurt causing me to have to walk the rest of the way home. Downstairs while putting on my capezios, I prayed, it was short and to the point. "God, I love you, may the words of my mouth and the meditation of my heart be rightful in your sight oh Lord my rock my redeemer. Please do not turn my heart to stone, if this is not over, I pray for strength, please heal my stomach, may your will be done. Amen. I opened my bible directly to proverbs three and started reading. I looked up saying, "Thank you for your word."

I started my warmups across the floor, there was a strength I have not felt in a while. I could not help but stop to look at my abs in the mirror. They were peeking through my tied-up top. Gently pulling my top up just enough to see most of my abs. My arms flexed as pulled my shirt up, they were toned and starting to show definition. I popped my hip out and looked at myself in the mirror paused for a minute and saying, "I hate you!"

Reaching for the mirror I used for spotting, I flipped it lightly, just enough to cause it to fall off the wall to the floor. Following the mirror to the floor, I fell to my knees not allowing myself to cry anymore, I hated myself, I lifted my hands and looked at my wrists and wondered, how quick would it be, would it hurt? Shaking my head "NO." Quickly going upstairs to clean, so Tammy would have her space, I could forget the thoughts I was thinking. I cleaned the bathroom, then went into Dave's old room and organized what was there. Once in boxes I stacked them neatly in mom's closet. Exhausted lying in bed awake for a long time. The room was dark, you could hear the noises outside and the occasional car drive by. My room started to spin so I got up and ran down the stairs. There were no lights on, just the lights from outside that provided just enough light for my eagle eyes to see.

I ran out the door, kept running until I reached the traffic circle outlining downtown. A fear came upon me like someone was chasing me, I kept running around and around the traffic circle, around and around, I started to panic; I was running for my life. I could not see his face, I started to yell "DAVE, DAVE, HELP ME, DAVE HE IS AFTER ME AND HE IS TRYING TO KILL ME. HELP ME, HE HAS A KNIFE. HE'S CATCHING UP WITH ME, DAVE HELP!" I felt a thrust from behind piercing my heart, I screamed, and I started to slow down. DAVE, HELP ME. I cannot run anymore, I screamed DAVE. My eyes closed, I had no strength left and was falling, at that moment Dave caught me and asked, "Autumn what's the matter?" I stuttered "He stabbed me, I am bleeding please, help me." tears were going down my face, Dave lifted me up, my eyes popped open. I looked around and I was in my room, it was a dream. I whispered, "What a scary dream." as I wiped the tears from my face with my blankets.

Still scared from the night before I did not want to go out, mom said that I could stay home to finish cleaning up before Tammy started to move her stuff in. Sitting at the kitchen table drinking coffee, I did not normally drink coffee, but I felt like maybe I needed it. My eyes were heavy, and I did not want to go back to sleep. The phone rang so I answered it, on the other end was a man's voice asking, "Can I please speak to Autumn Mayberry?" I said "Speaking." He said "My name is Constable Lundynski. I am with the Police department and I am looking for Cody Erickson, I have his last known address as one, two, three, one, two, thirty first street." "Is this your address?" I replied, "Yes." He asked, "Is Cody home right now?" I confirmed, "No, I haven't seen him. "OK, thank you." He said, the phone went dead. Mom asked, "Who was that?" Quietly I said, "A Private Investigator looking for Cody." Dramatically she said "Really, wow, that's weird!"

CHAPTER 12
Sent from above

It was a warm Spring day, the snow was almost gone, my heart was beating with anticipation. The news I just received needed to be shared with my teenaged friends. When Nancy and Patricia step off the bus from school I was there waiting for them, a smile lit up my face as I asked, "Do you want to hang out at the mall?" "I have something to tell you guys." Nancy quickly responded, "I have to go to work." Patricia said, "My parents asked me to watch my baby brother." Nancy tilted her head like a cat swallowed a mouse saying, "We have something to tell you as well, let's get on the bus before it leaves, we can tell you on the way home." We locked arms and got on the bus.

Sitting in the back seat, closely huddled, I said, "Go ahead, you go first." Nancy whispered, "Did you hear about Jeweler's?" Nancy got my attention "No." I said. Nancy went on to say, "We went to the mall at lunch it was crazy, everybody's talking. Three guys were in Breakfast All Day, having something to eat, they then went into the washroom, lifted the ceiling tiles, they all climbed up and crawled in the ceiling until they got to Jeweler's." "They cleaned the store out." "Rumor has it, that it is was Curtis, Luc, and Cody." My mouth dropped, I believed it. Patricia asked in a curious voice, "What did you have to tell us?" I said, "A Private Investigator called the house this morning looking for Cody, crazy right." Patricia said, "That's scary." I pulled the bell and walked to the door saying, "I'll call you later, Tammy is moving in today."

Tammy was at the house with the first load of her stuff. I went upstairs to see her and when she saw me, she smiled and went in for a hug and said "Yay, I am so excited." I smiled, "Is this all your stuff?" I asked. Tammy said, "No, I am going to my mom's tonight and coming back with the rest of my stuff tomorrow." "I have to go right now catch the bus; I will unpack later." I said, "I will go with you to the bus terminal." Tammy got on the bus to go to her Moms and I walked over to the Mall. I started to look around for some new pajamas, going down the escalator and a saw a boy named Steven going up. I know of him because a girl at my school is dating him. He was short, with dark hair halfway down his back, some of his hair covered his face, assuming to hide the foundation he wore, he had pimples and blackheads all over his face. he wore baggy jeans a white Adidas jacket that had red and black stripes down the arms and across the back and front. Steven smiled at me and said, "Hey did you see anybody up there?" I looked back and said "NO." and got off the escalator.

A few minutes later Steven was on the lower level, walking towards me. He nodded his head and said with a smirk, "Hey, you are Cody's girl." Steven did not stop walking towards me, before I knew what was happening I was stepping back to create space between us, he pressed his body against me pinning me to the wall, leaned in, his hand came up between my legs and he planted his lips on mine, sliding his tongue in my mouth gently saying, "Give me ten dollars." His hand reached into my pocket, taking my twenty dollars. Laughing he stepped back saying, "I'll be back in an hour. Meet me at the food court and I will give you your money." An hour past and Steve did not come back. I walked over to the bus terminal to see if I knew anyone there to borrow money to get home there was nobody, so I walked, I was starting to prefer walking anyways.

Tammy arrived the next day, my disappointment was buried deep, a stranger was going to be in my home again but, at least it was Tammy, someone from school and was my age. When she got to the house, we went straight upstairs and hung out while she unpacked. Tammy looked sad, I asked "How was your visit with your Mom, why don't you live at home?" Tammy said "I love my Mom, but I need to be away from her. I cannot talk to her. "She doesn't understand me." Rolling over onto my back to look at the ceiling I said, "I know the feeling." Tammy looked at me confused saying, "Your mom is awesome." To redirect the conversation, mischievously asking "Do you want to smoke a joint?" Tammy's face lit up, she nodded her head and said, "Fuck yeah!" Tammy took a tape out of her stuff and popped it into the tape player, while I rolled a joint.

The music started to play, and I had never heard it before, but the words sounded familiar. I asked, "Who is this?" Tammy said Club Nouveau, why do you treat me so bad." I said "OH." I finished rolling the joint and turned onto my back, intently listening to the rest of the song. This was the song that Cody sang to me that day at the bus terminal. I thought, why in the world would Cody, of all people sing this song to me. When the song ended, I asked Tammy "Are you ready?" She looked at me and pushed her hands up in the air and said, "Fuck yeah."

We walked down the stairs quickly and started to put our shoes on. Mom was at the kitchen table, "Where are you going?" She asked, looking at her annoyed, I answered in a snotty voice, "I am showing Tammy around." I flipped my head in the direction I was going and put my nose in the air, opened the door saying to Tammy "Let's go." Barely out the door, lighter in hand we lit the joint, inhaling with relief passing it back and forth. Tammy giggled, "Fuck we are going to get caught." Tammy quickly passed it back to me saying, "Someone is coming."

Marty was approaching us, I said "Hey Marty, how is it going?" Passing him the joint, he inhaled while saying, "It is going well, even better now, how about you?" I said "Good." He said, "Are you sure?" I quickly said "Yeah, this is Tammy she just moved in and lives with mom and I now." Marty nodded his head and said, "Hey," All three of us smoked the joint and walked back to the house.

Upstairs Tammy replaced the music with Ice Cube, Gangsta rap made me do it. I looked at her and asked, "What is it with your music?" Tammy looked at me surprised and said, "Do you think you can do better?" Proudly I said, "Definitely yeah." I got up, went downstairs into the living room and looked through the tapes until I found what I was looking for, I went back upstairs and took Tammy's crap music out and put in the tape.

John Denver, Thank God I'm A Country Boy. Tammy had a look of disapproval on her face. I started to lip synch and dance. I kicked my legs out then I did polka. I slapped my knee. Tammy laughed the whole time, then started to play the fiddle, jumping up saying, "Whoa, thank God I am a country girl." The song was finished, and I fell on the bed and laughed with Tammy. Tammy leaned back, looking all serious saying, "That fucking sucks." "I like it." I exclaimed. Tammy grabbed the pillow and started to hit me in the face. We laughed and I grabbed the other pillow and started to hit her. We hit each other until we could not do it anymore. Tammy looked at the ceiling and said, "That was the funniest thing I have ever heard, it made me hungry."

We walked to the store to get munchies and stayed up most of the night talking, I asked Tammy "Is there a boy that you like? Tammy said I like "Kyle Brooks, he is so hot." I grabbed the bag of salt and vinegar chips and offered some to Tammy. I asked, "Does Kyle know that you like him?" Tammy replied, "Yes I was at the bus terminal waiting for my bus and Kyle was standing right behind me. Paige pushed me into to him." She brought her hand up to her eyebrows and said, "How embarrassing, Paige blurted out she likes you." I laughed, "What did he say?" "He just smiled; his long eyelashes were flittering." The look on her face said she liked his response.

Tammy did not ask me about Cody, I felt flustered, angry, and scared, why couldn't anybody see me, and the pain I was experiencing? I was not able to talk about myself, what I was going through, or giggle about teenage things. I was fighting to wake up out of a reoccurring nightmare, all along being referred to as Cody's girl. Do I not get a say? The comforts of my bed were welcoming, which is where I stayed for a couple of days. Cody was in hiding; he could not risk coming here without the chance of being arrested for the robbery of Jeweler's. The intense stomach pain I have been experiencing have become mild episodes. I was able to pray and spend time with God, run and dance without Cody and the rest of the outside world trying to break me, I remembered what life was like before Cody.

Tom's mom went back up North to work at camp, allowing us to hang out again. Tammy and I met Nancy, and Patricia on the bus to go meet Bailey and Paige at Tom's. Tammy eyes got big and she brought her hand up to her mouth and saying, "I am going to be in so much trouble, I cannot skip school." Patricia looked at her and giggled, saying, "You can hang out for a while, then go get a note from the doctor, to excuse you." Tammy relaxed a little, but when we started to cut the hash up to do blades she kept saying "Oh, my gosh. We were not even high yet; we could not stop laughing.

We all took a turn then Bailey looked at Tammy convincing her, "Tammy, come do a blade." Bailey tapped the knives together and laughed. Tammy said, "I don't know." Bailey said, "Come on." Tammy got up and took the top of the pop bottle. Paige said, "Inhale when she touches the knives together." We all stood around watching to see what Tammy was going to do, she took a deep breath in, held the smoke for a couple of seconds then blew out, and sat down at the table.

Tammy did not say anything then she started to laugh. We turned and looked at her while she tried to keep a straight face, we laughed. Tammy's eyes got big, she put her elbows on the table, brought her to hands to her temples and said, "Oh my goodness, I am high, oh my goodness." We looked at each other not sure if she was OK? She started to rock back and forth, then sat up and took a deep breath in and said "Better." We gasped and paused for a moment waiting to see what was going to happen next. She started laughing, we joined in, Tammy tilted her head saying, "that is some crazy shit." We roared with laughter and continued getting high.

Tammy would not go to the doctor to get a note for school, she was too high, she said, "The doctor will know, will your mom phone the school saying I am sick?" "I can't miss school, or the association won't help me, and I have to go back home." I said, "We can say you were with me and we went to the mall, I am sure she will do it once." I phoned mom from a pay phone, she said that she would phone the school.

We stayed at Tom's well after supper and decided it was time to go home. I asked Tammy, "Can we walk?" My feelings about going home was not appealing to me at all. Tammy said, "What are you crazy, do you know how far that is?" I said "yeah, I have been walking to the Lake, then I run the rest of the way." Tammy looked at me like I was crazy, her arm came up, she flicked her wrist and pointed her finger saying, "You can run, I will catch the bus." I laughed saying, "We can catch the bus."

We got to the Lake bus terminal to transfer buses and stood there talking. I kept looking around to see if Cody, Curtis, or the white car were anywhere in sight. I could not help but notice a gentleman walking up to the terminal, I took a second look because he kind of looked like Phil Collins. He was about six feet tall and was wearing dark blue jeans, a blue dress shirt with a leather jacket. His hair was light brown and thinning. When we got on the bus we walked straight to the back and sat down. The gentleman that walked up to the terminal got on the bus, sitting on the opposite side of us. Tammy and I did not talk much we just looked out the window, when we approached the stop, we pulled the bell and got off the bus.

When we got home mom said, "Autumn that private investigator called again today looking for Cody." I looked at her annoyed, bobbed my head and in a snotty voice said "Oh." Walking right past her, acting like what she had to say was not important. Tammy looked at me confused because I did not mention anything to her about Cody. Mom asked, "What's wrong?" I just ignored her and went straight upstairs to bed.

It was hard to avoid the bus terminal, I hated going there, always watching my back to make sure I was safe, accept, I had to go to the terminal to get everywhere accept to work or Tom's. Sitting on the bench with my legs crossed, my transfer slip in my hand waiting for my bus, I kept watch of the buses pulling in, I wanted to see who was on them. Dakota and Kyle walking to the back doors of a bus as it pulled in. I thought, oh no, just sit here and hope that they do not see me. I kept my head down, not looking their way, I heard in a high-pitched squeaky voice call, "Autumn." It made the hair on the back of my neck stand straight up, I closed my eyes and quietly asking, "Please God keep me safe." I turned my head, smiled, and said "Hi." I watched them walk the gangster walk towards me, I would not take my eyes off Dakota, I did not trust him. Suddenly, I felt a blow to my face, I heard Dakota laugh "Ohhhhhh." I turned to see what the heck that was. Faith was standing over me saying, "Give me your bag bitch." She reached for my bag and started going through it. I looked at her with confidence saying, "There is no money in there, do you honestly think I would carry any money with me?" Faith grabbed my hair and slapped me in the face and said, "Fucking bitch." Faith let go of my hair demanding, "Give me your shoes." She reached down to grab my shoe off the foot that was crossed over my leg. I quickly stood up. She stood about eight inches taller than me, I met her eyes nodded my head no declaring, "I am not giving you my shoes." She ripped my transfer slip out of my hand defeated. She could not return my glare, just walked away like a dog with its tail between its legs.

I turned and looked at Dakota and Kyle, Dakota was talking to Kyle like what he had to say was more important and did not see what just happened. I asked them "Do you have sixty cents so I can catch the bus home?" Dakota giggled "Heeeha no, I don't have any money." Kyle pretended like I was not even there. My bus there, the front doors open, welcoming anybody that wanted to get on. I have never seen the bus driver before, he had brown hair and a beard, and he looked straight ahead. I said, "I am sorry I don't have any money; can I please catch the bus home?" He turned his head, smiled, saying "Yes, get on, I will take you home." I looked him in the eyes, but could not keep eye contact, unsure I should trust him. I sat on the seat directly beside him and faced him. He looked at me quickly saying, "I just need to change the sign." He flipped through some signage then the doors slammed shut and he pulled out.

I turned and looked out the front window of the bus, I could not help but notice he was going fast. I secretly peeked to see if there was anybody else on the bus, I was the only one, I was horrified, my life has been in the fast lane lately and I did not know what to expect. He sped past people waiting for their bus. I blurted, "You can let me off now?" I heard on the CB Radio a voice "Where are you?" He held his hand up and said, "One minute." The driver pulled the speaker to his mouth and pushed the button and replied, "I am on my way, I am making a quick stop." I heard on the other end "How long are you going to be?" He looked at me and responded "Five, ten minutes max." He placed the speaker back down, eyes on the road and sped on, I kept my eyes forward saying, "This is my stop up ahead."

The driver looked at me, his blue eyes softened, as he said, "I told you I will drive you home, where do you live?" I waved my hand through the air and quickly said "No, no, no, no, it is off route." He looked at the clock and said, "I am out of service, I have seven minutes." I looked at him relieved saying, "You have to turn left here." He turned left and looked at me and smiled. I returned the smiled and pointed, "Just right here on the right." Not taking my eyes off him. He stopped and asked, "Right here?" I looked at where he stopped, then back at him, nodded, and said "Yes."

The doors opened and I got off the bus in the parking lot beside my house. Turning to look at the driver "Thanks." He nodded, "I will wait here until I know that you are safe inside." I asked, "Are you driving this route now?" he smiled saying, "I am filling in for a friend." A little disappointed I said "Oh, Thank you." I turned and walked through the parking lot up the stairs. I turned back and waved. I waited for a moment to turn the handle, but the bus driver did not leave, the door opened, the driver yelled, "I am waiting." I could not help but smile, I opened the door and disappeared inside.

Closing the door behind me mom said, "Nancy called and wants you to call her." I grabbed the phone and ran downstairs and dialed Nancy's number. Nancy had call display and answered the phone "Hey, I was just leaving to meet Patricia on the bus, we are going to a movie tonight and are wondering if you wanted to go?" Pausing for a moment, thinking, that is just what I needed, a break from everything. I said "Sure, where is the movie at?" Nancy responded downtown. I am leaving right now." I said "OK." Nancy hung up the phone and I went upstairs, leaving the phone on the charger. Studying my face in the mirror where Faith punched me was a little red, so I applied some foundation, reapplied my mascara and lip gloss flipped my hair and ran down the stairs and started to put my shoes on. Mom asked, "Where are you going?" I glared at her and slammed the door.

We got downtown but missed the movie because we got high, I was just as happy to be sitting down at the tables hanging out. As we talked Nancy kicked me, I jumped, rubbing my shin saying "Ouch." Nancy whispered through her teeth, "Cody is here." I instantly panicked, I have not seen him in a while, and I did not know what to do. I tried to be discreet, whispering, "I need to go to the washroom."

I moved fast towards the washroom; I could hear footsteps behind me as I picked up the pace. The footsteps were getting closer, hearing Cody's voice "Autumn you slut." I slowed down by my head being yanked backwards. Cody said, "Where are you going you fucking slut, look at you." I stopped and turned around as I slapped his hand away. He looked at me as if I challenged him, I guess I did. I looked at him and said, "What do you want?" Cody looked me down from head to toe twice, saying, "You are looking pretty slutty, look at you, you are nothing but a fucking hoe, you are a slut." I flipped my nose up in the air and spotted the bathroom door and walked confidently towards it.

Once inside I stopped and looked at myself in the mirror, I did not see the same girl that stared back at me almost nine months ago, when I started grade ten. I took a couple of steps back and took a good look. The once baggy clothes to hide my developing body were replaced with form fitting clothes that complimented my body, almost to say, I am a grown up now, I was shocked! I said, "Come get it boys!" Anger came over me and I went through every single stall pulling the toilet paper until there was none left,

I kept releasing the handle on the paper towel dispenser until that was gone, turning on all the water taps, and started throwing all the toilet paper and paper towel in the sinks. What did not fit in the sinks I threw in the toilets and did not flush. I walked back to the sink looking at myself the whole time, grabbing the saturated paper, throwing it against the mirror, screaming, I did not want to see my reflection in the mirror. There was so much paper, I covered the ceiling, walls, and the mirrors. When that was done, I went from bathroom stall to bathroom stall filling the toilets and making sure that the walls were covered in tissue. I fell to my knees, lifted my hands and said "God! I don't know what your plan is for my life, but I know I am not a prostitute." I took a good look around at my masterpiece, got up off my knees and walked out the door feeling satisfied.

When I got to the table Cody was being the charming, handsome, grown, eighteen-year-old boy that he thought everybody knew and loved. I quickly said, "I am leaving, there is nothing here." Nancy and Patricia looked at me and quickly and agreed "Yeah, let's go." We walked to the escalator and I took one last look at Cody as he stood there, flipping my hair as if to say these are my girls. Cody stood at the upper level watching us as we went down the escalator and disappeared through the mall to catch the bus.

I was so distracted and confused on the bus home, I sat by the window looking out wondering, why Cody would hurt me so bad? This stranger that I did not know, force his way into my life and then repeatedly do hurtful things. I murmured "God, what did I do?" Nancy asked, "Autumn are you OK?" I nodded and looked at her, saying "Yeah, I am good." My stomach was hurting, and my heart was heavy, my whole body ached. Why won't this end?

Turning to look back out the window still able to see Nancy and Patricia's reflection I said in a partial laugh "I can't wait to get a good night's sleep."

Tammy was not home when I got there, mom tried talking to me. I walked straight into the kitchen to make something to eat and ignored her. She asked me "Why do you hate me?" I looked at her almost shocked that she would even ask me that, how dare she. I could not stand looking at her anymore, going straight upstairs to my room and slammed the door. saying, "I hate her." I threw myself on my bed and screamed into my pillow, that is where I stayed.

I had that scary nightmare again, quietly going down the stairs in the middle of the night turning the music down low, grabbing a pillow and a blanket, I sat on the floor and started to read my bible. Slowly moving to my side, I crunched the pillow, so it supported my head. I moved the bible so I could still read it. Tammy woke me in the morning "Heyyyyy." My eyes opened and I smiled. Tammy asked, "Why are you down here?" I was stiff as I sat up saying, "I had a nightmare, then I couldn't sleep, so I just came down here." Tammy asked, "Do you want to come with me to the mall?" I need some make up." I was hesitant I started to shake my head 'Hmm." Tammy said, "Come on, I will buy you a drink, it will be fun." What I wanted to say was, will you protect me from getting beat up? What came out of my mouth was, "OK!"

Orange Julius is where we stopped first to get a drink before Tammy went to get makeup. The Mall was oddly quiet, I noticed that gentleman I saw at The Lake bus terminal was walking towards us. Moving in closer to Tammy I nudged her, Tammy turned around to see what I wanted her to see. The gentleman was right there saying, "Autumn, I am Constable Lundynski, I am looking for Cody, do you know where he is?" I said, "No, sorry I don't know where he is." He looked around and said "OK, thank you." I watched him walk away, he looked like he was on a mission, he kept stopping, it was obvious he was looking for something or someone. Tammy went to Pharmacy Mart to get her makeup, I had no money, so I waited outside the store on the bench. Tammy paid for her things and we left.

Across the street Constable Lundynski was leaning up against a parked car looking in our direction. I nudged Tammy saying, "Don't stare but Constable Lundynski is standing over there in the parking lot." Tammy pretended to laugh, turning her head, questioning, "Wow! What did Cody do?"

CHAPTER 13
Zulu

My nap was interrupted by the phone ringing, mom said "Autumn, the phone is for you." Handing me the phone. I said "Hello." There was a man's voice and he said, "Hi Autumn my name is Constable White, I am phoning to let you know that the charges you pressed against Brandy have been dropped." I asked "Pardon?" He repeated, "The charges against Brandy have been dropped." I said "Why." He said, "The charges were dropped, and I am just letting you know." "OK." I said. He did not offer any more information, he hung up and I stood there. Mom asked, "Who was that?" I pretended she was not there.

Tammy quickly followed me up the stairs, asking "Autumn, are you alright?" I nodded my head and said "Yeah, I am leaving, I am going to walk to work today." Tammy watched as I got my things together hoping to get something as to why I was upset. It was not just the charges being dropped against Brandy. I cannot be anywhere including my own home without some sort of threat. Abruptly storming out of my bedroom, down the stairs, glancing back at Tammy I said, "I am going to Tom's after work if you want to meet me." I forced a smile and left.

I got to the lake and sat on the bench, looking at the water, it was so peaceful. Trying to remember a time when I experienced peace and when I felt safe. I sat back closed my eyes. The ponds behind our house, where Lisa and I used to play in the barefoot looking for tadpoles or frogs. We walked along the side of the water splashing each other, saying you are going to get warts. The sun would light the curls on Lisa's long hair. I opened my eyes and saying, "A time when I had no cares. Breathing in deeply, taking one last look at the lake and said, "That was then." Pushing myself off the bench and started walking.

The sky was overcast but it was still a warm day, I always felt better when I was outside in the fresh air, warm breeze on my face. I kept looking down at my feet, steps turned into jumps, crack to crack on the sidewalk, chanting, step on a crack break your mother's back. I looked up and saw Bailey's house, so I crossed over the street and got to the apartments between Bailey's and Tom's. The grass was turning green and the little hills distracted me to look at the strategically placed trees between the hills. I turned to look in front of me, I jumped when I heard "ZULU!" Looking up Cody was standing right there, where he come from?

I froze for a moment and gasped, deciding what I should do, I turned the other way and started to run, Cody's words chasing me, "What's the matter Autumn?" "Why are you running?" He caught me, turned me around, pulling me in until he was firm against my back. Grabbing my hair, he pulled my head back, putting a knife to the right side of my neck, saying, "What's the matter bitch?" I should just kill you right now." Pressing a little more pressure to my neck with the knife. I tilted my head back further affirming his threat, stating, "Go ahead, you have already taken everything I had." I wanted him to do it. The knife still against my neck, closing my eyes as the knife lingered, Cody threw me to the ground. I fell on my hands and knees, Cody throttled me, grabbing my hair, pulling my head back, then using the knife, he started to cut my hair. My head bobbing as I watched the pieces drop to the ground beside me. Cody stopped cutting my hair, flinging my head forward. Unsure what was going to happen next, I stayed still for a moment. Unsure if I should move, slowly I turned and looked to see what Cody was doing, I could not see him. Pushing myself back on my knees, slowly looking around, still no sign of Cody, he was gone.

Looking down on the ground in front of me, I stammered, "Do not cry, do not let him see you cry." My hand shaking, I picked a piece of hair up, feeling my hair. On the verge of tears, I murmured "Don't let him see you cry." I closed my hands and rubbed my fingers over the hair, and I watched it fall back to the ground. I stood up and took a good look around, but I could not see Cody, I looked in every direction as far as I could see he was gone. I stayed there for a moment waiting to see what was going to happen next, unsure if I should stand still or run. Cody did not come out, so I cautiously walked the rest of the way to work.

I went straight to the bathroom to see how bad my hair was, half my hair was gone in the back, and part of the top. I dug in my bag and pulled out a hair pretty, pulled my hair back in a ponytail to see if it was noticeable. It looked like a bad haircut put in a ponytail to try and hide it, where it was cut stood straight out. It was getting harder for me to look at myself in the mirror. I tried to see who was staring back at me, I could not see me, I would not recognize myself if it were not for my two different colored eyes staring back at me. I moved closer to stare this person down saying, "He should have just killed you; I really wish that he would have!" "No, He is not going to break you." "Be strong." I bowed my head saying, "Please God, Please, help me, why is he doing this, you never let me down." Taking a deep breath in, "You can do this." I walked up to the front counter and asked the girls "Is the cart counted and ready?" No eye contact was made, one of the girls responded, "All counted ready to go." Grabbing the cart and started doing my coffee run. Customers were so happy with my performance they were tipping me all night.

I passed by the scene on my way to Tom's, we were smoking a joint when Dakota showed up with a couple of guys, acting all gangster like, every second word from their mouths was, "Zulu." I got up and left as quietly as possible, holding my shoes in my hands, closing the door behind me, running to seven eleven stopping outside the doors I slipped my shoes on. I bought a pack of cigarettes and asked the clerk, "Could you please call me a cab?" He said "Sure." My heart racing while standing in the back of the store waiting for the cab.

Once home, I went straight to the bathroom and pulled my ponytail out and turned the shower on. I washed my hair to see what it was like freshly washed. It looked horrible, as I tried pinning my hair back in different styles Tammy knocked on the door and asked "Autumn, are you there?" Replying, "Yeah I will be right out." I pulled my hair back and went and laid down beside Tammy on the bed in my room, falling asleep while Tammy was talking. The sound of voices and laughing woke me up. I got up and slowly walked down the stairs, two black men sitting at the table with mom and Tammy. Getting a closer look, I could see that they were rolling a joint. Mom said, "Autumn come here." I could tell that mom had been drinking, she was loud and laughed a lot. Hesitantly, standing beside her at the table. "This is my daughter

Autumn, guess what, I can find her in a crowd full of people, she has two different colored eyes," As she slurred her words. I studied the men as I said, "Hi." Mom pointed at the two men and said, "That is Nick and that is Peter."

Nick Smiled and said, "Hello" he was tall and looked very pleasant. Peter was shorter which made him look heavier, he did not smile, his eyes shifty, he nodded his head and continued to roll a joint. My senses were off the charts with him. Mom said, "they are from Montreal." I turned and looked at mom saying, "I am going back to bed." Unable to sleep with the stranger's downstairs, I laid there for a while, my heart was racing thinking about the knife Cody held to my neck.

Tammy was blow drying her hair when I got up in the morning, she was getting ready to go see her mom. Tammy said, "Good Morning, you were tired." Asking, "What are you doing today?" I said, "I am going to work out." Tammy asked, "Do you want to meet me at the mall after I visit my mom?" I said "Sure, what time?" Tammy said, "It's nine right now so about two o'clock." Saying, "I can do that." I got up and grabbed my workout clothes and got changed.

I came back from my run and went downstairs and started my stretches and praying, I took a deep breath in and exhaled. I opened my eyes and Cody was standing in front of me. I slowly moved to stand up straight. Cody said calmly "Autumn," As he raised his voice, "Where is my passport?" "I don't know." I trembled. Cody moved in closer, looked me in the eyes and said, "I Love your eyes they are so beautiful, something about those eye's" "I am not joking; I want my passport and I want it now." Cody's eyes looked empty, like I was looking in a tunnel with no end. I would not let him see my fear. Cody said, "Get my passport, NOW!"

Going up the stairs, Cody followed. Pushing the chair up to my closet, I moved the clothes and reached for Cody's passport. Reluctantly handing it to him, Cody snatched it out of my hands and said, "Downstairs I want to talk to you." I stepped down off the chair and Cody pushed me to the stairs. Cody right behind me, his hand tight on my arm pulling me through the kitchen right past mom saying, "I need to talk to Autumn." He opened the door to basement, saying, "Downstairs." I went downstairs, Cody put his passport in his pocket and his bag on the floor.

Cody walked over to the tape player and took the tape out of the player, he turned and looked at me, took a tape out of the pocket and held it up for me to see. He placed it in the player and pushed play. It did not take me long to figure out it was Cher, if I could turn back time. I stood there listening for a moment as Cody walked towards me, he put his hand by my ear and gently moved towards my chin and said, "Listen." He kissed my cheek and started to undress me and turned me around, guided me to the bed, positioning me as I was the day before.

When Cody was done, I laid there beside him as he stared at the ceiling saying, "I never wanted to hurt you." Turning his glance to me. "If I could turn back time I would." I nodded, Cody put his arm around me asking, "You believe me, right?" I turned my head not saying a word, I did not know how to answer that. Cody said, "I will always be a part of you." I did not understand what he meant, I laid there for a moment trying to figure it out, finally saying, "I have to go and meet Tammy." I sat up, Cody grabbed my arm, "If I could change the past I would." I yanked my arm, got dressed and went upstairs for a shower.

I felt defeated, the shower running, sitting on the edge of the tub wondering aloud, "God why will he not just leave?" I felt the water and turned it hotter, my clothes falling to the floor like rags as I stepped into the shower to wash Cody's filth off me. Clenching my fist as I stated, "God I cannot stand him." I turned the shower off, my back to the mirror as I wrapped a towel around me. Cody was gone, he took his bag with him, my heart said that was the last time he was going to be there, not sure it will be the last time I see him though.

The bus was pulling up and I could see the driver, it was the bus driver that drove me home a couple of days ago. The bus came to a stop and I stepped up and showed my bus pass and sat on the front seat so I could see him, saying, "Hello." He kept his eyes forward as he pulled away returning the greeting, "Hello." "I just want to say thank you for driving me home the other day." He nodded his head while saying, "No problem." I watched out the front window as the bus headed towards the bus terminal. As the bus pulled up, I saw Tammy standing in the bus shelter. I smiled and said "Bye, have a good day, thank you again for driving me home." I heard "You are welcome," as I walked off the bus.

Tammy met me outside. As she approached me her face looked like she swallowed a bird. Concerned I asked, "What's wrong." Tammy said loudly and quickly "You are not going to believe it, Constable Lundynski has been here at least three times walking through the terminal and then back to the parking lot, in and out of the parked cars." "Is he looking for Cody?" I looked around, the terminal was empty, like everybody knew Constable Lundynski was scoping out the Terminal saying, "I don't know."

Tammy and I started to walk to the mall, just leaving the platform of the terminal, I heard "Autumn." Looking, it was Constable Lundynski walking towards us, stopping in our path, saying, "Autumn, there is a girl that got beat up, the girl who did it fits your description." I thought, boy are your wires crossed, pausing I said, "Well it wasn't me." He kept looking around, I knew that feeling, I did it all the time, he was looking for Cody, distracted he said, "OK, thanks if you hear anything let me know." As he handed me his card, looking at I said, "OK." I watched him walk back to the parking lot. Tammy and I turned to walk to the mall, I whispered as we walked, "Yes, he is definitely looking for Cody."

Dakota and Kyle were at the Mall in the Food court when we arrived, Tammy saw them and did not hold back telling them about Constable Lundynski scoping the bus terminal. Dakota got scarier every time I saw him; I have only saw Kyle a few times. I nudged Tammy to stop talking, asking, "Don't you need to pick up a few things?" Tammy brought her hand up and snapped her fingers together and said, "We will see you guys later." As she bobbed her head side to side, I turned and walked away annoyed.

I sat outside on the bench and waited for Tammy, Dakota and Kyle were walking towards me, I heard Cody's voice, "HEY!" My hair stood up on the back of my neck, I hated that voice, I turned my head slightly and looked, Cody was standing down the hall. He stood there for a second and began to sing as he tapped his foot. "You knock me off of my feet now baby, Whoa." I looked around and there was nobody else around but Dakota, Kyle. He started to dance towards me and said, "Come on girl." I stood up and started to walk towards the doors of Pharmacy Mart, Cody ran and blocked my path signing, "Hey pretty baby with the High heels on you give me fever like I never, ever known." Cody thrust his hips into me. Dakota and Kyle stood there laughing.

I ran past him into the store and found Tammy and said, "Tammy Cody is out there, let's go!" Tammy asked, "Did you tell him that Constable Lundynski is looking for him?" I said, "AH NO, are you coming?" She said, "Yeah I just need to pay for this." We left the store and they were gone. I examined the stores as we passed by, there was no sign of them. I could not look at myself in the wall to ceiling mirrors, I was walking so quickly Tammy said, "Hey slow down, what is your hurry?" I said, "No Hurry." We got outside I slowed down as we walked to the terminal. I said "Tammy, our bus is here." We took off running, as we approached, I saw It was my bus driver. We stepped up and I sat down in the front seat, Tammy said, "Let's sit in the back." Standing my ground, saying, "NO." There has only been one time that I felt safe throughout all this, that was when I was on this bus, sitting right here, with this bus driver. He must have been sent from heaven.

Tammy decided that she did not want to go home yet, so she said, "I am going to stay on the bus and go back to the mall to see who shows up there." I said "OK." "Are you going to see if Kyle is still there?" Tammy smiled and brought her hand to her mouth, looking embarrassed "NO!" I said, "I will see you later."

I got off the bus and went home, my shoes were not even off, mom asked, "Do you have any smokes?" I nodded my head as I said "Nope." She quickly pleaded, "Will you go get some?" I dug the money out of my pocket and threw it on the table and said,

"Go get them yourself." I went straight upstairs and turned on the music, Club Nouveau Why you treat me so bad was playing. I rewound the song and threw myself on the bed, as I listened to the song I thought about Cody and how the past nine months have been a reoccurring nightmare, the reflection in the mirror confirmed it, Covering the mirror was not an option, it did not change how I felt inside, I teared up as thought about my promise to God, that I would wait, how could I face him? How would he know that I tried? My tears started to fall uncontrollably.

After surviving the first heavy rainfall of the flood I went downstairs to get a drink of water, mom pleaded, "Autumn can you please go and get some smokes?" I did not budge, "NO!" "Autumn, why do you hate me so much?" Mom asked. Months of anger built up inside of me came out and I shot arrows at her saying, "WHY?" "Why do I fucking hate you so much?" "You fucking stupid bitch." I yanked my ponytail and started to run my hands through my hair, saying, "Look at me!" "This is why I fucking hate you." I grabbed some pieces of what was left of my hair saying, "This is your fault." I stormed over so I was standing in front of her saying, "You fucking stupid bitch." "You invited Cody into our home, he stalked me, raped me, and gets his fucking hoes to beat me up and steal my money." "You fucking let boys in that Cody sends to have their way with me." "THAT IS WHY I FUCKING HATE YOU." "Look at me, I am a fucking whore because of you. Not only do you let it happen, you fucking watch it." "That is why, I fucking hate you."

Mom sat there with no expression on her face, like it meant nothing, finally spewing, "Your fucking arse, you don't know whether it is punched or boarded full of holes, I didn't do nothing,." Turning her head as she took a drag of her cigarette. I stormed upstairs and rewound the song again and turned it as high as it would go. I sat on the edge of my bed staring at an unrecognizable reflection. I attacked the mirror; I smashed my fists against the hideous reflection. I swiped all the makeup off my dresser, I tore down all the clothes hanging in my closet and raged through my drawers, throwing everything on the floor. I wanted to stop the pain, I wanted it to end, I fell to the floor exhausted.

I stopped, softly whispered, "You can end it, you don't have to feel anymore." I ran to Mom's room and found her razor blades, went back to my room, rewound the song again, recalling everything leading up to this moment. Shaking as I held the razor blade in my right hand lifting my left wrist. I started to make light strokes just enough to break my skin and start bleeding. I grabbed the razor with my left hand and started the same thing on my right wrist, it did not hurt. I closed my eyes and said, "Just go deeper." I took a deep breath in.

I jumped when mom yelled "AAHHH, What the hell do you think you are doing." She stormed over and grabbed my left hand with the razor with her good hand and said, "You want to fucking die, do you need some help?" "Let me fucking help you." She was forcing my left hand holding the razor towards my wrist, I screamed "AAAAHHHHHH." She let go, the razor fell to the floor, in a high-pitched voice. I screamed "I FUCKING HATE YOU!"

I ran into the bathroom and locked the door, slid down the wall, curled up in the fetal position and pleaded "God make it end, I can't go anymore, please this hurts too much, make him stop." I pulled myself off the floor my, but I could not stand straight up because of the pain in my stomach. I muttered "Deep breaths, deep breaths." I made my way to my bedroom and grabbed my sweater and pulled it over my head, picked up my bag and walked down the stairs, put my shoes on and walked to the bus stop, I couldn't help but smile when I saw my bus driver.

Blonde, the tide is high was playing at Tom's. Patricia, Nancy, Bailey, and Paige singing as they sat at the table with Tom. They all said 'Hi.' Bailey asked, "Autumn do you have any drugs?" Reaching into my pocket pulling out what was left of the gram of hash I bought from Kaleb, handing it to Tom to roll a joint, singing, New Kids on The Block, Step by Step as we did blades. Tom lit a joint and passed it around.

The atmosphere changed when Dakota and his brother Jamie showed up, looking out the window to see if Cody was hiding in the background. My stomachache became intense, trying not to show the pain. Jamie said, "Hi Autumn, how are you doing?" "I haven't seen you in a while." I said, "I am good." "How are you?" He smiled and said, "I am good." I always liked Jamie, even in junior high he was always nice to me. My stomachache would not give me a break though, I cut the conversation off by saying, "I have to go."

Tammy was sitting at the kitchen table with Nick and Peter when I got home. Nick asked Tammy and I, "Do you want to go out for a drive?" I jumped at the opportunity to leave for a while. I said, "Yes." Tammy smiled and said, "Fuck Yeah." We got in the car and Peter drove to the downtown area, pulling to an apartment building, we followed him in. Nick lit a joint and we all sat there smoking it. When it was done Peter put it out and grabbed Tammy's arm and said, "Come here, I want to show you something." Tammy said, "No, show me here." Peter pulled her up and started to drag her out of the room, Tammy was almost crying, "No, No, No!" Unable to move, frantically I looked at Nick. Nick reached into his wallet and pulled a picture of a beautiful black girl and said, "This is Iesha my girlfriend." Nick went on about how much he loved her and could not wait to see her and that he was only here for work. "I want to marry her." he said. I did not hear anything in the other room, it was quiet. Tammy and Peter both came out of the other room, Peter said, "Ok, let's go." Tammy had a look of horror on her face, but never spoke of what happened behind that door, I did not ask, I knew what had happened. The car ride home was quiet.

CHAPTER 14

I Surrender

Waiting at the bus stop my feet had to keep moving, stepping side to side, I felt very anxious and could not help but look around for Cody. The bus pulled up and it was a different driver, but I did not care, I just wanted to get home. I bolted up the steps to the seat beside the back doors in case Cody got on the bus. sinking down in the seat so it would look empty. I peeked over the seat to see where I was, I pulled the bell, the bus stopped, and I darted home.

Over the next few days my bus driver was driving the bus in the mornings, so I made sure that I was going home in time to make his last round on the route. I sat on the front seat talking to him I did not get his name, but it sure felt nice to be safe. If Nancy and Patricia were on the bus, I still sat up front, they never asked any questions. I have not heard from Cody, and Constable Lundynski stopped calling the house and hanging out at the mall. People were starting to show up at the terminal again, that included Dakota and his creepy friends. Tammy liked to go just to see Kyle, she would get all silly and laughed a lot when he was around.

Nancy had a serious look on her face one night at Tom's, we were sitting down at the table. Nancy took a drag of the joint and passed it to Patricia as she blew the smoke out, she looked at me asking, "Did you hear?" "Hear what?" I asked. Nancy said, "You didn't hear about Cody?" My anxiety started to come on and Paige passed me the joint, I quickly inhaled then exhaled, took another drag, held my breath then passed it to Patricia. I blew the smoke out asking, "What about Cody?" Nancy said, "Cody is going to Vancouver." I said "Oh." "When is he leaving?" Nancy said, "I do not know when, I just heard that he was leaving to Vancouver." I did not know what to say, relief and excitement was washing over me, thinking, could this be over?

With the news that Cody was leaving for Vancouver I thought my stomachache would be gone, it was too for me to take, I could not lay down, stand up, sit, or walk, the pain was great and getting worse. Taking deep breaths did not helping either, I was stuck on the stairs grabbing my stomach. "What is wrong?" Mom asked, In between my breathing and cramps I managed to say, "I don't know, my stomach hurts." Mom asked "Why?" I wailed "OUCH, I started breathing deep breaths, throwing in, "I don't know." I tried to get down the stairs and I could not, Mom said, "I am taking you to the hospital." I stayed on the stairs until the cab arrived, he came in helped me out to the cab, practically carrying me.

The cab pulled up to the front doors of Holy Hospital, the driver got out and helped me into the doors and left. The nurse at the front desk came running with a wheelchair asking, "Are you in labor?" I could not speak only breath, the pain was too bad, my cramps were really close together, I shook my head No. She sat me down in the chair and took me straight in and told mom to fill in my paperwork.

The nurse wheeled me upstairs and helped me on the bed, palpated my huge stomach. I did look like I was pregnant, ready to give birth, no wonder she asked. The doctor came in with mom and started asking me questions. I keep saying no in between my cramps. I yelped "Ouch." A few minutes later a nurse came in and said, "Here take these, it will help you with the pain." She handed me the pills and held a cup of water for me to take. I popped the pills in my mouth and drank the water. The nurse said, "I will be back in a few minutes."

About ten minutes past by and the pain started to disappear. The doctor came back and looked at mom and said "We are going to run a few tests and keep Autumn overnight. Mom nodded her head and said "OK." The doctor looked at me and said, "The nurse will be along in a couple of minutes." I did not make eye contact and just nodded my head. He turned around and said to mom "You may as well just go home, and we will let you know. The Doctor left and I said, "Mom just go home and get some rest." Mom said "OK." She asked, "Do you have money for a cab?" I reached in my pocket and gave her some money and she left.

My stomach was still bloated, and I had a sudden urgency to have to go to the bathroom. I went and sat down just in time, I lost all control and felt my stomach relax. I sat there for a moment then got in the shower and enjoyed the peace and quiet. I changed into the hospital scrubs and hopped into bed and fell asleep. I awoke to Nancy and Patricia standing beside my bed, Patricia asked "Autumn are you OK?" "What happened?" I told them everything but the washroom ordeal. Nancy asked, "Are you feeling better?"

I said "Yeah." "Do you want to go for a walk?" They said "Sure." We walked around for a while and then Nancy said, "We should go." I said, "Thanks for coming." and went back to my room.

In the morning I heard talking, Mom and the doctor were standing outside the door. They both came in, the doctor said, "Good news Autumn, everything looks good." "How are you feeling?" I said "Better." He said, "You can go home now." I said "OK, Thank you." I changed into my regular clothes and left the hospital feeling better.

There was a gift and a card with flowers on the table when I got home. Mom said, "That is for you, from Dave." The flowers were a combination of pink and yellow carnations, baby's breath, and tiger lilies, I took a deep breath in saying, "WOW, they are beautiful." My eyes started to swell up will tears as I picked up the card and read it. Sorry to hear that you are in the hospital, wish I was there, love Dave, and Dana. I pulled the card to my chest and thought, I wish you were here too. I quickly picked up the present so I would not cry, it felt flimsy like material. I opened the happy wrapping paper and held up a nightie. My first thought was how did he know I needed pajamas. It was a white nightie with short red sleeves, on the front it had a bear with a night cap wearing green and white striped pajamas sitting up in bed with the blankets pulled up. The print almost looked like a child colored it, the writing said love me tender. I smiled asking, "Who brought this?" Mom said, "Dana did." I have not met Dana yet, and Dave did not talk much about anything. I always did most of the talking when he was around.

I went upstairs and quickly changed into my new pajamas, I loved them. I came downstairs and asked mom "Do you want some toast?" Mom said "OK." I poured a tall glass of milk and sat down and ate my toast with peanut butter and jam with my milk. The phone rang and I ran to the phone and said "Hello." It was Dave. I said, "Thank you for the cards, flowers and pajamas, I love them." Dave could not talk because he was on a break and had to go back to work. I thought it was because he would start to tear up, I said "OK, I love you and thank you." He said "Yup, I love you too." in his strong masculine voice he uses when he is emotional and does not want to show his true feelings. He hung up the phone and I held it for a moment before I hung it up.

I stayed in bed all day, in between dozing off I read my bible and prayed. Tammy came home and I do not think I ever saw her this happy, I could not help but smile, intrigued I tried to listen attentively. She had a good visit with her mom, and she saw Kyle. Tammy leaned in saying, "I am pretty sure Kyle likes me." She raised her hand to her mouth and giggled.

Life was starting to feel somewhat normal again, I could catch the bus and not worry about seeing Cody, I am excited that he is leaving for Vancouver, I will never have to see him ever again. I could not remember the last time I went anywhere that I wanted to and did not have a sense of fear. I stood up to get off the bus at the terminal to meet Tammy after school, Tammy was already there. It was nice seeing her happy. When Tammy saw me, she said, "Heyyy!" I smiled, we started talking, Tammy nodded her head for me to look behind me, I turned around to see who was there, Surprised, Cody stood about a foot away from me. I gasped, I felt myself shaking as I stood there. Cody's face had no expression, his eyes were empty. He said "Autumn." He had a black jacket on, his left hand grabbed the zipper as he slowly opened his jacket to reveal a knife. The blade was about ten inches and the handle dark. I felt like everything was happening in a slow-motion.

Cody closed his jacket saying, "You are coming with me." He grabbed my arm and pulled me as he walked towards the bus to go downtown. He whispered, "Don't do anything stupid, get on the bus now." I nodded and said "OK." He followed me on the bus and said, "Go to the back." Walking with my eyes down, not wanting to make eye contact with anybody I sat down on the back seat. Cody said, "By the window." I slid over and Cody sat beside me, leaving no room to move. Looking over at Tammy who followed on the bus, sat on the opposite side of the seat, beside the window, staring outside, was she oblivious as to what was happening.

The bus started to pull out of the Terminal, turning my head to looked out my window, wanting to get a good look where we were going. My mind wondering if that was the knife Cody held to my throat and cut my hair with? I occasionally looked over at Tammy and she was content and happy staring out the window looking at everything go by. It was rush-hour, and the bus was not moving as fast as it would have been if there was less traffic. We were approaching the core of downtown, Cody reached up not giving me any breathing space I had to tilt my head, he pulled the bell and said, "This is our stop."

The bus came to a stop and Cody stood up and waited for me to go in front of him. Stepping off the bus we stood in front of the college, the building looked so big under the grey sky. Cody grabbed my arm and pulled me, saying, "This way." We headed west until we got to the end of the campus Cody yanked on me, saying "This way." Walking north back in the direction we just came from.

Cody got to an apartment building and opened the door, we stood in the entry way, Cody firmly said, "Up the stairs," He followed us. The apartment had an old dirty smell, what once was white walls looked all dingy and yellow, the carpets were so dark I could not make out if they were gray or blue. We walked up one flight of stairs and Cody opened the door to go down the hallway, it was so dark that I looked to see what little light there was, where it was coming from. There was no light except from the exit signs. Cody walked down to the middle of the hallway and opened a door on the right.

Tammy went into the apartment before me, Cody came in behind me. The apartment was bright, there were two rooms that I saw. The first one directly when you came in had a large window on the right and a bed against the wall under it. Past that room was a larger entry way with patio doors directly ahead. I stood there scared. There were four other people there. Curtis, who sat on the right in what looked like a chair from the dining room table, the chair was in the corner facing the wall directly across. I could only get a side profile of him. His eyes looked directly ahead of him with his head high. His black curly hair looked like it was freshly cut, he did not look in our direction. He wore a white t-shirt with med blue denim jeans and legs stretched out in front of him, he did not move.

Luc stood left of him, looking directly at me as he took a couple of steps towards me. Kyle was standing in the middle of the room. Tammy looked at Kyle and said "Hi." as she walked into the next room allowing me to focus on Jamie, he stood on my left, I could read the fear in his eyes when he saw it was me, he moved around nervously and quickly looked towards to patio doors.

Cody grabbed the back of my hair, tilted my head, kissing my neck. I said "Don't." and tried to move but could not, his grip was too tight. Cody then started to kiss my neck again, letting go of my hair, whispering in my ear "Come on baby, one last time for old time sake." I turned, pulling away, looking him in the eyes, firmly saying, "NO." Cody tilted his head, smirking when he said, "Fine have it your way." My eyes could not help but follow his arm as he lifted it up, stretching it out beside me, snapping his fingers.

My eyes focused, I was shocked, Luc grabbed Tammy's hair, pulling her towards him. Kyle started to knee Tammy in the stomach and elbow her on the back while Jamie kicked her from behind. Whipping around to look at Cody, fear in my eyes, nodding my head and saying, "OK, ok make them stop, please make them stop." Cody nodded his head, they stopped. He moved towards me and put his hand between my legs and started to rub while he kissed my neck. I moved away and said "NO." My head followed my eyes as Cody moved his arm and snapped his fingers in the direction of Tammy.

Curtis did not flinch, still seated in the chair, staring at the wall. Luc and Jamie were having a tug of war with Tammy's hair while Kyle kept punching and kicking Tammy. I could see the look of distress on Tammy's face as she yelped and screamed "AHHH, OUCH." I turned to Cody and said in a scared voice, "OK, Yes, I will, just make them stop, please." Cody nodded his head and it grew silent. I turned and looked at Tammy, Cody grabbed me and started to touch me and kiss me, yelling with urgency, "TAMMY YOU FUCKING STUPID BITCH!" "WHAT ARE YOU FUCKING STUPID?" "FUCKING RUN NOW!" Tammy bolted, I watched her run out the door.

Cody grabbed me, dragging me to the entryway of the next room, and yanked me around. Not able to make eye contact with any of the four in front of me. Cody's left hand had a grip on my right arm and his right hand reached across in front of me, ripping my blouse off, standing there exposed, I pleaded with a pure heart, "God this is not your will for my life, falling to my knees face down praying.

Lord, I am here to meet with you, I want to see your face again, take me to the most holy place.

MAJESTY!

It was well into the night and the battle between light and darkness was present, spiritual warfare surrounded me. Behold, there was war in heaven: Michael and his angels fought against the dragon; and the dragon fought and his angels and prevailed not; neither was their place found in heaven. And the great dragon was cast out. There was peace in the heavens. Frozen unable to move, I was flat, face down when a strong, powerful, voice from heaven said, "GET UP" "NO!" I said in a determined voice. "I am never going to forgive her!" Thinking it was about time, fix this, take me away. Hoping for some type of response, or direction, now what, anything, there was nothing. I waited and thought, am I dead? Knowing I was in the presence of my Abba Father, I felt peace.

Finally, with my heavy arms barely strong enough to lift myself up. I stumbled a couple of steps to lean against the tree, realizing where I was. I frantically looked all around me, dawn was on the horizon, the tears started to roll down my face uncontrollably. Through my tears I cried "Thank you God." I took one last glance around and ran.

Knowing that we came in from the south, deeper downtown was the very direction I wanted to avoid, chances are greater he would be there. The other option was north, the direction would take me home. Dodging down the street, it was unfamiliar, the bright lights from the busy street ahead directed my way. Lord be a light onto my path and guide me. I gasped, "That's it, I have seen this street before." I turned right, feeling scared, my breathing was so hard, my heart beating so fast I thought it burst my chest.

The tears stopped, fight or flight was roaring through my veins. My legs began to get more and more strength as I ran as fast as they would carry me, I did not look back. I felt a cool breeze, stopping briefly to zip up my jacket. "Oh yeah," I whispered out loud as I fumbled with the zipper to cover my nakedness. I did not have time to think about it, I must get out of here, before he finds me. Traveling east I saw a big light that said Stone Furniture. "Yes!" I said with relief, that is where I get on the bus.

Approaching the busy street, I saw that the traffic was low, unaware if it was safe to cross, I bolted. Suddenly I heard a screeching noise and a horn as I leaped onto the curb, a car just missed me. Hoping that the buses were running I waited anxiously, stepping from side to side. "Please be running." My eyes could not help but look around and behind me, I whispered "what if he sees me?" "God please, please don't let him see me." I looked in the direction of downtown, "Yes, there is the bus, please hurry." I looked up "God Please don't let him find me please, please get me out of here and home safely."

The bus was slowly approaching, I spit on my fingers and wiped under my eyes, just in case I had makeup down my face, then I used the inside of the jacket to wipe my face. The bus stopped, the doors flung open, I jumped up the stairs inside the bus. Not making eye contact with the bus driver, embarrassed and scared, I pleaded "Please, Please I have no money I need to get home!" The bus driver asked me "Do you need to transfer? "Quietly replying, "Yes, please." He ripped off a transfer slip and handed it to me. Unable to look at him directly I said "Thank you. "As the bus started moving, I turned and walked to the seat beside the back door just in case he got on the bus, hoping I would have help from the bus driver to escape quickly.

My heart was beating out of my chest as I sat down on the warm seat, leaned up against the side of the bus looking out the window. The bright lights of downtown passed by quickly, the store lights dim and flickering or not working. I was so tired that my eyes wanted to close. The travel time on the bus was about thirty minutes away from home, then I can finally sleep in my own warm bed.

I felt a jolt and my head bobbed up as I gasped, the bus came to a stop. I must have dozed off and was dreaming that I saw him. The bus driver opened the door and then got off the bus, lit a cigarette and stood there smoking it. The bus driver threw his cigarette on the sidewalk and stepped on it, he hopped back on the bus. My transfer bus pulled up, getting up I walked to the door asking, "Could you please open the doors and let my off?" The doors opened and I got off the bus, I paused for a moment to take a good look around. I though it looks safe to go, without any further thought I walked across the terminal to the bus. The door opened, I held out my transfer slip and walked to the back of the bus. I sat in the corner, pulled the jacket over my knees, and slid down with my knees up on the back of the seat in front of me. "He will never see me here." I whispered.

My heart still beating fast, the bus pulled away. I lifted my head to look where we were on the route. "I am just about home, thank you!" I whispered. I turned and looked out the window I saw the houses with lights off. I thought of all the people in their safe warm beds, and the wonderful dreams they must be having. As we approached the fields, I pulled the bell to get off at the next stop. Thinking it is probably safer to go a different way home through the newer subdivisions and pathways and not be seen, even though it was longer.

The bus stopped just before the new subdivision that did not have streetlights yet. I looked around and sighed with anxiety saying, "You are almost home." Quickly making my way through the streets, onto the familiar pathway behind my house, almost daylight, I was so close to home, I could see it creeping up in the distance, looking further than I knew it was. Some of the houses have lights on, people are starting their day, mine just ending.

With heavy legs stepping up onto the steps of the house, turning the handle quietly hoping mom was asleep. I closed the door and made sure the door was locked. I leaned against it took a deep breath in and thought am I having a nightmare? A tear rolled down my face. I told myself "it is ok, you will never have to think about it again." I crept upstairs and turned the hot water on in the shower, unzipped the jacket, it fell to the floor as I got in. The hot water touched my body like a massage, at first a little intense, then my muscles started to relax. It felt good to be able to shower, any dwindling thoughts about what happened washed down the drain.

I walked to my bedroom and pulled out my underwear and nightie, slipping them on saying relieved, "Love me tender." My cozy comforter was so inviting. I pulled back the comforter crawled in and snuggled up with it. I sighed ahh, this feels so good, I closed my eyes took a deep breath in, I fell into a deep sleep and slept until the next morning.

Stages of Grooming.

Stage 1:   Targeting the victim
Stage 2:   Gaining the victim's trust
Stage 3:   Filling a need
Stage 4:   Isolating the child
Stage 5:   Sexualizing the relationship
Stage 6:   Maintaining control

The adolescent brain is not equipped to react or understand what is happening.

The journey has not been easy for Autumn, her mom continued to try and prostitute her out until she was eighteen. Not only was her promise to God broken, but her heart as well. Displaced, used, abused, left in the wilderness. Most nights, crying herself to sleep, so much internal shame that was not hers to carry. Autumn was angry at God, wondering why he would let this happen, thinking she was used goods, never going to be good enough, but God says otherwise.

Matthew 11: 28,29 - Come to me all you who are weary and burdened, and I will give you rest. Take my yoke upon you and learn from me, for I am gentle and humble in heart, and you will find rest for your souls. Going forward Autumn believed God was a God who was who he said he was, the only high Autumn experienced in Church, was the high of being in the presence of God.

Finally the dream of becoming a bride happened, she married an amazing, kind, and gentle man. She danced with her best friend, he taught her how to capture beautiful moments on film. When apart she experienced love always through the love letters found in random places, fresh flowers at all times to remind her how beautiful she was to him. Soon the laughter was shared with the little feet running through the hallways giggling, "Daddy come find us."

One Halloween the dance ended, and they cried. His tears stopped, hers did not. Family and friends surrounded her, again Autumn was again face down on her knees crying to God looking for a reason why it had to end. Autumn prayed for a husband, as a lily among thorns, she awaits for her Beloved.

Matthew 6:33 KJV - But seek ye first the kingdom of God, and his righteousness: and all these things shall be added unto you.

Psalm 37: 4,5 KJV - Delight thyself also in the Lord: and he shall give thee the desires of thine heart. Commit thy way unto the Lord; trust also in him; and he shall bring it to pass.

Without the divine love of her family, friends, and God, Autumn never would have heard the words of God saying, "It is time." One thing that will always remain.

Romans 8: 38, 39 - For I am persuaded, that neither death, nor life, nor angels, nor principalities, nor powers, nor things present, nor things to come, nor height, nor depth, nor any other creature, shall be able to separate us from the love of God, which is in Christ Jesus our Lord.

Romans 12:19 KJV, Dearly beloved, avenge not yourselves, but rather give place unto wrath: for it is written, Vengeance is mine; I will repay, saith the Lord."

Deuteronomy 32:35 KJV, to me belongeth vengeance, and recompence; their foot shall slide in due time: for the day of their calamity is at hand, and the things that shall come upon them make haste.

There are two things in this world we are not allowed to discuss, religion and politics. Please note I hope you read the fine print of your contract of employment, you may or may not have a term for employment that states

Any discussions concerning religion and politics at work is strictly prohibited, this is cause for immediate termination. On the spot.

There are two women in the bible, Revelation 12, the woman of Israel, the women clothed with the sun and the man child. She brought forth the man child, who was to rule the nations with a rod of iron, and her child was caught up to God and his throne.

Revelation 17, the Harlot of Babylon arrayed in purple and scarlet color, and decked with gold and precious stones and pearls, having a golden cup in her hand full of abominations and filthiness of her fornications. She represents sex, power, and money, and the kings/rulers, political governs of the world, are riding on the scarlet colored beast.

Revelation 19: 7, 8, 9. 10 KJV - Let us be glad and rejoice, and give honour to him: for the marriage of the lamb has come, and his wife has made herself ready. And to her was granted that she should be arrayed in fine linen, clean and white, for the fine linen is the righteousness of saints. And he says onto me, Write Blessed are they which are called into the marriage of the Lamb. And he saith onto me, These are true sayings of God. And I fell at his feet to worship him. And he said onto me, See thou do it not: I am thy fellowservant, and of thy brethren that I have the testimony of Jesus: worship God: for the testimony of Jesus is the spirit of prophecy.

Revelation 22: 6, 7 KJV - And he said unto me, These sayings are faithful and true; and the Lord God of the holy prophets sent his angel to shrew unto his servants the things which must shortly be done. Behold I come quickly: blessed is he that keepth the sayings of the prophesy of this book.

In the name of Jesus, may all glory, praise, and honour be to God, Amen!